TW-123

The Proper Care of
TARANTULAS

Ann Webb

Photo and illustration credits: David Alderton, William B. Allen, Jr., Dr. Herbert R. Axelrod, E. Balon, D.T. Boujard, Paul Carpenter, Dr. Guido Dingerkus, Pedro Antonio Federsoni, Isabelle Francais, Paul Freed, Michael Gilroy, John Hancock, Alex Kerstitch, Ken Lucas, Christine McNamara, Dr. Sherman A. Minton, Alcide Perucca, Ron Reagan, Ivan Sazima, Dennis Toulson.

1995 Edition

Distributed in the UNITED STATES to the Pet Trade by T.F.H. Publications, Inc., Or T.F.H. Plaza, Neptune City, NJ 07753; distributed in the UNITED STATES to tt Bookstore and Library Trade by National Book Network, Inc. 4720 Boston Way, Lanha MD 20706; in CANADA to the Pet Trade by H & L Pet Supplies Inc., 27 Kingst Crescent, Kitchener, Ontario N2B 2T6; Rolf C. Hagen Ltd., 3225 Sartelon Stre Montreal 382 Quebec; in CANADA to the Book Trade by Vanwell Publishing Ltd., Northrup Crescent, St. Catharines, Ontario L2M 6P5 ; in ENGLAND by T.F.H. Public tions, PO Box 15, Waterlooville PO7 6BQ; in AUSTRALIA AND THE SOUTH PACIF by T.F.H. (Australia), Pty. Ltd., Box 149, Brookvale 2100 N.S.W., Australia; in NE ZEALAND by Brooklands Aquarium Ltd. 5 McGiven Drive, New Plymouth, RD1 N Zealand; in Japan by T.F.H. Publications, Japan—Jiro Tsuda, 10-12-3 Ohjidai, Saku Chiba 285, Japan; in SOUTH AFRICA by Lopis (Pty) Ltd., P.O. Box 39127, Booyser 2016, Johannesburg, South Africa. Published by T.F.H. Publications, Inc.
MANUFACTURED IN THE UNITED STATES OF AMERICA
BY T.F.H. PUBLICATIONS, INC.

The Proper Care of
TARANTULAS

Ann Webb

ACKNOWLEDGMENTS

My most grateful thanks to my husband, Frank, who helps and supports my every endeavour and puts up with a lot! My thanks to my good friends Paul Carpenter, John and Kathleen Hancock, Christine McNamara, Sue Clarke, Dennis and Carol Toulson, Andrew Smith, Vince Hull-Williams, Virginia Cheeseman, Sarah Brook, Tony Balchin, Roy Dunn, Ralph Fitchett, and last, but by no means least, John Nichol. Without these wonderful people I could not have produced this work.

Dedicated to "CLEO" —
My Favourite Mexican Red Knee

Contents

ABOUT THE AUTHOR

Ann Webb was born in the early years of the second World War, the eldest of two daughters of Queenie and Albert Bastable. She was educated at secondary modern school in her native East London/Essex borders and spent her early working life as a secretary, accountant and writer of fiction. Devoted to animals, this is her second book on tarantulas. She is married to Frank Webb, a retired newsagent; they live in a pleasant modern flat in Hertfordshire with their collection of tarantulas, scorpions, snakes, fish, geckos and terrapins. They complete their mini-zoo with a dog called 'Nikki', a cockatiel called 'Wally' and three cats.

Introduction

For many years, talking about tarantulas has been taboo! Taboo mainly because the mere word 'tarantula' conjures up a vision of huge, deadly spiders stalking the earth, killing or threatening anything and everything that moves. This is a complete fallacy since the majority of tarantulas are peace-loving, silent creatures! The thought of actually having such a creature in one's home has never even been contemplated by the average pet owner. The shock-horror idea of spiders (tarantulas in particular) is accentuated by the media and film makers, serving to further scare off potential tarantula pet keepers. But just look at a tarantula; see how beautiful it is and how wonderfully some are coloured. How can something that has so much attraction to the eye be frightening?

In reality, people have been keeping these creatures for many years, albeit mainly for scientific study and research. Now, however, the age of the tarantulas has surely arrived and we can indeed talk about them! So let's do just that.

The popularity of this amazing and

Curly Hair Tarantula

fascinating creature is three-fold: (i) the said amazement and fascination; (ii) the small financial expenditure needed to keep the spider; (iii) the minimal space the spider needs—therefore the ideal pet for a small house or apartment.

There are some 30,000 species of spider in the world, of which some 700+ are theraphosids (tarantulas). In fact, the large hairy spider we all know as a tarantula is misnamed. The real 'tarantula' is a small wolf spider (*Lycosa narbonensis/Lycosa tarantula*) coming mostly from southern Europe. This was prolific around the town of Taranto some 200 or so years ago where the terrified inhabitants believed the bite, if not lethal, was certainly enough to cause madness. To that extent thus, if bitten, they would perform a frenzied dance to rid themselves of the poison. The dance was the Tarantella; the spider became the tarantula. Now that 'tarantula' is in such common use, it would be very hard to change to the correct term—theraphosid— for these large and very attractive spiders.

For myself, I am fascinated by all animal life but I became

Brachypelma smithi.
Mexican Red Knee Tarantula.

involved with tarantulas almost by accident. We were searching for a small pet to fit in with a small house and, as I mentioned before, the tarantula suited the bill perfectly, never forgetting that a surname like Webb also matched with the spider!

At that time, I had no intention of increasing my collection beyond that one spider, but these creatures are addictive! Initially we, as do many others, believed that tarantulas basically consisted of the beautifully marked Mexican Red Knee (*Brachypelma smithi*), but we quickly discovered many other strange and

wonderful—not to mention DIFFERENT— species of tarantula.

In the course of this book, I shall elaborate upon the differences between the species, some quite dramatic, which I hope will help the pet keeper and potentional pet keeper to decide upon the tarantula best suited to his or her needs. Remember though, whichever you choose, you must be prepared to make a commitment to caring for the tarantula for its life. Too often do we find that a pet (and not just

Note the distinct red markings on this tarantula's legs which led to its name—Mexican Red Knee.

spiders) is bought solely for the pleasure it can give to the owner, with little or no thought to the welfare of the animal and what happens to it when the novelty wears off. Of course we must gain pleasure from our animals, but this should not be the prime consideration. The animal's welfare must be paramount.

My personal love for and involvement with animals goes back to childhood. I cannot recall a time when my family did not have a dog about the house. Cats came later, as did rodents, birds, fish, terrapins, hermit crabs, giant land snails and snakes. The spiders arrived somewhere in the middle of this lengthy list of animals with whom I share both my home and my life, but the spiders do take first place now for, as a child, I was terrified of the smallest house spider! These days, in many instances, I prefer the company of my animals to that of the destructive *Homo sapiens* (man).

In this introduction, I must emphasise that the pages which follow are based upon my own experiences with tarantulas. Learning about them being a

This picture shows a tarantula's biting ability. No matter how calm your pet may seem, remember that he has the ability to bite if provoked.

An aquarium tank set up for tarantulas.

very gradual process, of course I have made mistakes. Fortunately, no spider has suffered at my hands because of my lack of knowledge, and the mistakes have been educational. The problem was, in the beginning, that there was no correct information available about these creatures. The few books one could get were sparse in their contents so that caring for such an exotic animal was very hit-and-miss. No one, not even the dealer, knew much about them, and misinformation (which flowed prolifically) was far worse than no information. Misinformation was all that could be had.

Today, thanks to a hardcore of dedicated arachnologists who have been willing to share their experiences and impart their acquired knowledge to others, tarantulas as pets will have a far better chance of survival in captivity than they had when I started with tarantulas in 1981.

Above you will have read the word 'arachnologists'. For those who do not know, spiders are all arachnids, as are scorpions, mites, ticks

Argiope sp. Its common name, amongst many, is 'St. Andrews Spider' because of the thick lines in the web in the shape of the cross on the Scottish flag.

and solifugids. We get the word from Greek mythology. The Lydian maiden Arachne competed in a weaving contest with the Goddess Athene. Arachne won the contest and enraged the Goddess so much that Athene forced Arachne to hang herself from her own silk before turning her into a spider so that she would perpetually weave webs. Therefore we have 'arachnids' (spiders), we have 'arachnologists' (those involved in the care, study and research into spiders), we have 'arachnophiles' (those who love spiders) and we have 'arachnophobics' (who are, of course, those for whom spiders hold only terror and disgust).

So, let's talk about tarantulas! Are they of different temperaments? Are their characters different one from another? Quite simply, the answer is yes! Between the species there are radical differences and even between individuals of the same species characters clearly vary. Get to know YOUR spider and you have achieved much.

This book will allow the reader a closer understanding of the nature of the

Female orb-weaver spider looking over her food.

theraphosids (the tarantulas). My own experiences and those of my close friends and fellow arachnologists are the facts upon which I have drawn my text.

With the disappearance of natural habitats, e.g., rainforests, and over-collection to satisfy the needs of the purchasing public, it is becoming much more important to captive breed even the more common species. Worldwide, there is sufficient adult breeding stock available in captivity to make the plunder of the wild a thing of the past. It is also being debated that at some stage captive-bred

Aphonopelma **sp. Tarantula.**

A Curly Hair Tarantula,
Brachypelma albopilosa.

tarantulas may be returned to the wild, but this is, of course, in the future. I am not averse to collecting wild breeding stock of new species, provided control is exercised. Certainly there may well be species of tarantulas as yet undiscovered, and the search for these should, and I am sure will, continue.

Extensive captive breeding programmes are underway in the UK, including that of the BRITISH TARANTULA SOCIETY, and there is little doubt that as captive-bred spiderlings come onto the market, life in the wild will be preserved to a great

Tarantula with shed skin.

Brachypelma smithi, Mexican Red Knee.

extent. The only worrying point is that to many buyers the large, colourful hairy spider is the attraction, and rearing up a miniature version which looks nothing like its adult counterpart does not appeal. This is a pity since, in my opinion, there is nothing more rewarding than bringing up 'baby', watching its development over its formative weeks and spotting colour changes as it becomes first juvenile, then subadult and finally adult.

It is important to recognise, more to accept, that a tarantula—whether wild-collected or captive-bred—is a wild animal and should be respected as such. No matter how docile you may think your specimen to be, you must never lose sight of the fact that she/he has all the necessary equipment to bite and will certainly do so if provoked.

I hope that this book will appeal and that it will give the pet owners and potential pet owners help, guidance and encouragement.

ANN WEBB
Radlett, Hertfordshire
England

Brachypelma albopilosa, **Honduras Curly Hair Tarantula.**

**Complete skin shed by a
Red Knee Tarantula.**

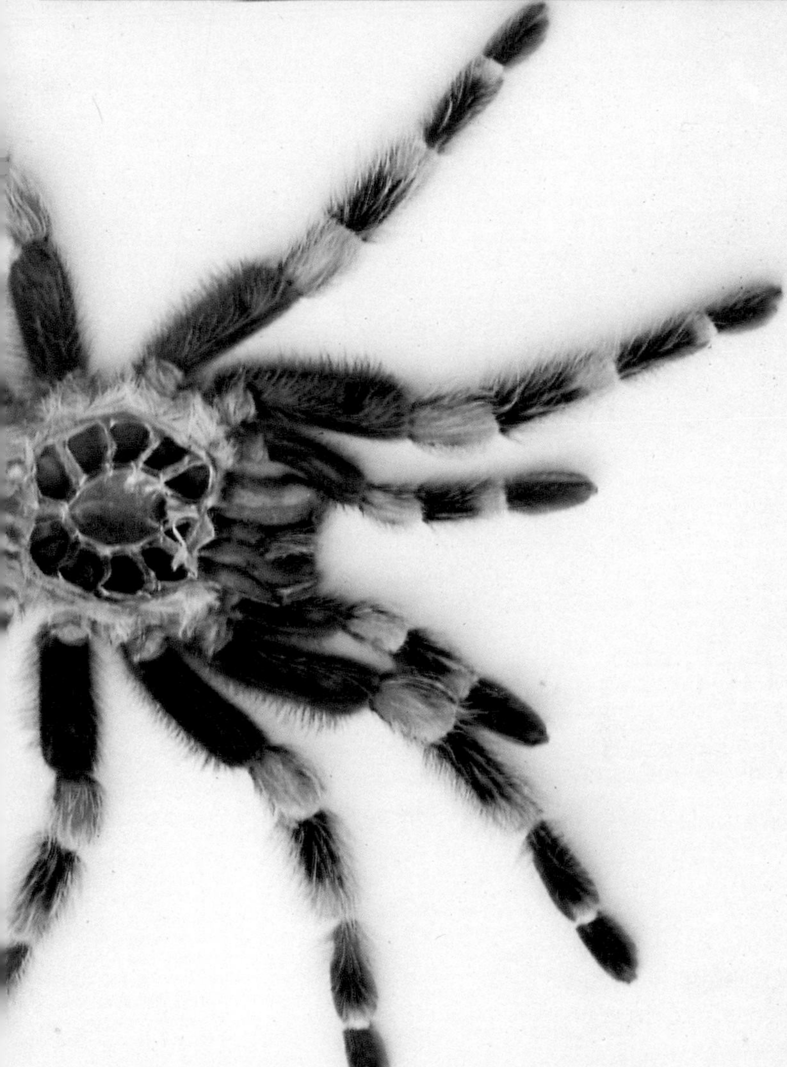

A tank layout suitable for tarantulas.

Basic Keeping

When we first think of keeping an 'exotic' pet we should always ask ourselves one very important question. WHY? There are, no doubt, many reasons, but the worst by far is the sensationalism: The show-off who likes the idea of possessing something that few if any of his friends have; the person who intends to terrify friends and relations with this 'lethal' spider. Tarantulas are a prime example of sensationalistic clap-trap. There is nothing the media enjoys more than to play upon this side of spiders—the worst offenders being, undoubtedly, the newspapers. Tarantulas are, of course, most definitely exotic and our motives for keeping such a creature in captivity in our homes must be the very best possible.

I, for example, keep spiders for four basic reasons: (i) I love them; (ii) I feel they are badly misunderstood; (iii) I want to do my best toward their preservation, particularly in the wild, thus preventing their extinction; and (iv) I like to study their habits, their individuality, their beauty, their grace and their very special lifestyle.

I am often asked

what they do. Really, the answer is—not very much, since, particularly during the day, they move rarely. At night they seem to be more active, but I have known a tarantula to remain stationary for days on end. From that aspect they are, perhaps, uninteresting to people who like an active pet. For myself, one of their more appealing traits is that they are so undemanding. When the dog barks for 'walkies', the cats scream for food or the cockatiel screams just

for the sake of it, I really find the peaceful lives of my spiders behind the curtain in the dark a comfort!

The most vital thing is, of course, their preservation, captive breeding being far more important today than ever before. These spiders are really the dinosaurs of the arachnids (Andrew Smith 1986), being exceedingly primitive. If they are not bred in captivity, then there is little doubt they will go the way of their

Above: Brachypelma smithi, the Mexican Red Knee Tarantula. *Opposite:* The moulted skin of a tarantula is the spit and image of its owner.

gigantic co-habiters of the Earth millions of years ago. Data collected thus far tell us that there are, probably, 700+ species of tarantula in the world but, having said that, new species ARE found from time to time. The disappearing rainforests, which are the natural habitat for approximately three-quarters of the species,

are causing much damage to their ecology. We cannot put back the forests that have already been lost but we can work to prevent more carnage. In any event, the damage that has been done can only be acceptable if specialist captive breeding of tarantulas is undertaken.

Remember the rule of thumb in the *Introduction*: the furry creature you have in the corner of your living room is a WILD animal. It will bite if it feels the need, and it is totally unpredictable.

So, before you dash out and buy a tarantula, consider the decision very carefully. You will have the spider for anything from 2-30 years, depending upon species and gender, and you MUST be prepared to give it the attention it needs during its lifetime. While, obviously, a spider is in no way as demanding as, say, a dog, it is nonetheless part of the household, a living creature that is dependent upon YOU, the pet owner, for food, water and care— everything it needs in captivity that it gets naturally in the wild, you must provide. Do, therefore, think about it seriously before dashing headlong into a relationship that may prove to be more difficult than you realised.

Get advice from those who know, and

Brachypelma sp., the Flame Knee Tarantula.

there are experts throughout the world, including the British Tarantula Society, the British Arachnological Society, the Spider Club of Southern Africa, etc. In fact, there are arachnological bodies in all corners of the world and information often is available in libraries, natural history museums and zoos. I strongly recommend that you join a society when you are contemplating buying your first spider, not after you have bought it and made all the mistakes! If you do it right from the start, then you and your tarantula will live in perfect harmony. I guarantee that once you have taken the plunge and become involved with tarantulas, the interest will be firmly cemented and you will want to know more and more and to keep more and more! I started with one spider and, currently, have around 80!

A Texas Big Bend Gold Carapace Tarantula.

Basic Housing

Now that you have made the decision that a tarantula is to come into your life, you should, if you are sensible, provide the habitat before the spider arrives.

Many people labour under the misconception that tarantulas need lots of space. A completely false impression. Basically, they need to feel the walls of their home in close proximity. In the wild,

ABOVE: *Pamphobeteus sp.*, more commonly called a Colombian Giant Bird Eater. **OPPOSITE:** Small plastic terrariums make ideal cages for a tarantula. They are lightweight, easy to clean, and easy to close securely. Photo courtesy of Hagen.

a tarantula digs out a burrow which is enlarged as the spider grows. If the tarantula is a female, she rarely strays away from the burrow, lurking at the entrance to await passing food! She will admit males only for mating purposes, and if they do not quickly make good their escape, they will meet the ultimate fate and become her next meal! The male tarantula, once mature, will wander in search of a mate but only relatively short distances. A stroll of two feet across the carpet is like running the London Marathon! Ergo, it follows that if you house your pet tarantula in a small fish tank, either glass or plastic (10"x8" maximum) and give it a suitable substrate upon which to walk, the spider will readily accept this as its burrow. Be absolutely certain that the lid is firmly fixed and cannot be raised by the spider. These creatures are very good at escaping so that soft plastic lids are not really suitable unless they can be weighted down sufficiently to prevent egress.

Tarantulas are not in the least gregarious and MUST be housed alone. If two tarantulas are put together they will at best fight, and at worst will kill each other. Therefore, it is definitely not cruel to keep the spider on its own. You can of course divide a larger tank into two or even three sections provided there is absolutely no chance of the inmates scaling the divider to invade each other's territory. A good way of fitting a

Although this terrarium provides sufficient cover, the substrate will not allow digging of even the most simple burrow. Burrows allow the tarantula to live in very dry areas by increasing the humidity.

divider is by using plastic runners with a sheet of glass cut to the correct size and slid into place. For some aquariums you can purchase a commerically made divider.

Wherever you locate the tank in your lounge or animal

room, be very careful that sunlight cannot cross the tank, especially the morning sun. The tarantula has eight eyes (four for daytime vision and four for nighttime), but these are very poor in visual quality and bright light is a severe irritant. The ultraviolet rays are equally dangerous and can cause desiccation. A tarantula will always dig down or retreat into a corner to avoid bright lights of any description.

Substrate. Here the lack of correct information at source of supply is responsible for many early deaths. The ideal substrate is a horticultural medium used for bringing on seedlings in nurseries, namely vermiculite; peat can be used as an alternative, but vermiculite is far and away the better medium. A mixture of peat and vermiculite is sometimes used, especially for large spiders such as the Goliath Bird Eater (*Theraphosa leblondi*), but avoid sand, gravel, stones, rocks, etc., which are strictly forbidden and a very dangerous addition to a tarantula's tank.

When you place the substrate in the tank, be sure it is very moist. Vermiculite, when you bring it home from the garden centre, is very dry, so the first thing to do with it is to moisten it. Cut the top off the bag

Theraphosa leblondi, **Goliath Bird Eater.**

and place the bag under a slowly running tap issuing warm water; by piercing tiny holes all over the bags, excess moisture can be easily squeezed out. The substrate should be fairly moist but not running in water.

Landscaping your tarantula's home can

be a soul-destroying task since the inmate will inevitably change it, or even destroy it completely, and undo overnight your labour of love and artistic mastery! For adult and subadult spiders I therefore suggest a substrate 2" to 5" deep. If you cut a new plastic flowerpot in half this makes an ideal burrow that can be covered with substrate to disguise it. The spider may or may not use this depending upon mood, but it does serve to enhance the tank layout. Sphagnum moss or snake grass will help to keep up the humidity,

This illustration displays the use of a half flowerpot as a burrow.

Brachypelma emilia, Mexican True Red Leg.

and I have found that spiders like to lie in the moss; in some cases it serves as camouflage, e.g., in the case of the Mexican True Red Leg (*Brachypelma emilia*).

An open water dish

is the only other furnishing needed. Fresh water should be given daily. If you decide to use plant life in your tank, NEVER choose cacti, which can damage a spider severely, even fatally, should the spider fall upon or brush against it. The ideal plant would be one of the plastic varieties. However, plants are really unnecessary and, whether plastic or natural, will without doubt be uprooted by the spider at some time or another.

The habitat described above is suitable for all ground-dwelling or terrestrial spiders.

For arboreal, or tree-dwelling, species, the tank needs to be tall and slim. This can be custom-made quite simply to, say, 12" tall x 6" wide. Substrate, again preferably vermiculite, should be 5" deep; twigs or a piece of cork bark placed upward at an angle will act as an anchor for the tarantula's tube web that will be constructed with great skill and precision. Many arboreal spiders spin tube-like webs that are extremely thick and in which they live, moult, feed and lay their egg sacs. The webs are used as a nursery for the spiderlings until they disperse. Water dishes are not, as such, necessary for the spiders, although they do need to drink. The best method of giving water is to spray the web and the bark daily so that the tarantula can take on liquid more naturally.

under the tank are one method. Light bulbs are another. Some keepers use ceramic hanging heaters or ground-based hot rocks; others

Heating has long been the subject of great debate and differences of opinion among arachnologists. Heating pads placed

Hapalopus incei. **The Trinidad Olive Brown Spider—a small spider but a prolific web builder.**

Aquarium tank fitted with a ventilated lid.

use heating cables. My personal preference is to utilise the central heating in the house; my collection is kept on racks strategically placed, with a curtained front to give the spiders the darkness they prefer. I have found from experience that adult and subadult tarantulas, no matter what species, survive quite happily at a temperature of 70° to 75° Fahrenheit, the temperature at which our room is constantly kept. Let us, nonetheless, discuss the different types of heating more thoroughly.

1) Heating Pads

These are very efficient, available in outputs of 10-15 watts and, placed under the tank and controlled by thermostat, will keep the tank interior at a constant temperature once set correctly. These pads are ideal with arboreal tarantulas but not so good for ground-dwellers and burrowing species. Heat, as we all know, rises, and often a burrowing spider finding itself too warm will dig down (frequently to the tank bottom) to cool off. If a heating pad is provided, instead of coming into contact with a nice cold surface, the tarantula meets only yet more heat. Therefore this method is perfect for heating arboreal spiders living aloft in their webs.

Ceratogyrus darlingi, the East African Horned Baboon. Note the unusual hump (or horn) on the carapace.

2) Light Bulbs

If placed inside the tank these are a useless danger for tree spiders that, inevitably, will build their web nest around the bulb, using it as an anchor. Even ground-dwellers climb from time to time, so a light bulb inside the tank must be positioned so that the spider cannot touch it. One of my close friends, Dennis Toulson, has successfully solved this problem by inserting the bulbs through the hood sides and placing a glass 'false ceiling' beneath the lighting. This has the effect of throwing the heat downward, deflecting it onto the substrate. As stated, this is very successful. Dennis uses a two-foot tank divided into two sections, making economical use of the facilities available.

Recently, a method being widely used is a small flexi-top table lamp outside the tank. The light (and therefore the heat) is directed onto the tank and moved away if the temperature rises above the correct setting. This too can be connected to a

C.J. MᶜNAMARA.

Above: Aphonopelma seemanni, Costa Rican Zebra.

Opposite page: Haplopelma minax, Thailand Black Tarantula.

thermostat if required. In either event, the light bulb used MUST be red or blue since bright lights are an irritant to the spider's poor eyesight. Light bulbs can have a drying effect which could lead to desiccation if placed inside the tank without the glass protection, making vital even more attention to humidity.

3) Ceramic Hanging Heaters

These are rather expensive and, once again, I do not recommend these for arboreal spiders. Once installed, the spider will often use the heater as an anchor for the web-nest. I have even heard of a tarantula who spun her nest in which to lay her egg sac around the heater, with many problems ensuing.

Equally, ground-dwellers could climb up and come into contact with such a heater with disastrous results.

4) Hot Rocks

I have no personal experience of these but I wonder whether a spider climbing upon the rock could be burned.

5) Heating Cables

This is a method widely used by those with more than one spider tank to heat and has proved very successful. The cables are manufactured in loops that can be placed on a foil-lined

trough, say, 6 feet in length, covered with either peat or vermiculite. Five or six tanks can then be set upon it. The cable is thermostatically controlled and can be set to the desired

Since most tarantulas are nocturnal, they should not be left in nearly barren terrariums for long. Such stress may cause illness.

temperature. This method of heating is suitable for any species of tarantula, adult or subadult, ground-dwelling or arboreal, since the cables leave 'cool' patches in the substrate. Logically, of course, this method would not be of use to the person with one spider.

6) Room Heating

For those with larger collections, this method is far and away the most economical. As aforementioned, most adult and subadult tarantulas will survive happily between 70° and 75° F, and if your house has central heating then obviously this can be most cost effective. Otherwise a space heater or oil-filled radiator or night-storage heaters can be employed very successfully. Again, all these can be controlled thermostatically for maximum economy.

Humidity is a vital aspect for a tarantula's well-being and can be easily achieved provided the tank is no bigger than specified.

Make sure that the substrate is thoroughly dampened when placed into the tank. The heat within and the open water dish will assist in keeping the humidity at the desired levels (see individual descriptions for the relevant percentages) and can be supplemented by spraying the tank sides as necessary. Condensation on the tank sides cannot be avoided, but an easy method for cleaning the front tank wall so that you can observe the inmate is to use a magnetic aquarium cleaner. I do not recommend that you leave this in place when not being used since climbing spiders can dislodge these

Most pet stores carry a variety of accessories that may be used to decorate the terrarium.

cleaners and damage themselves.

I have mentioned desiccation on several occasions throughout this text, and some species of tarantula are more prone to this than others. In particular, the *Avicularia* species of South American tree spiders, which include the South American Pink Toe (*Avicularia avicularia*), need very high humidity. Desiccation (which is, in simple terms, the drying out of the

A few nice plastic plants, readily available at pet shops, will improve the appearance of your terrarium. Photo courtesy of Hagen.

internal abdomen) is a main killer for this species. An easy explanation of desiccation is to compare it to a natural sponge. Brought onto land and allowed to dry out, the sea sponge will crumble, and if you try to rehydrate it you have an impossible task. This is precisely what happens to the spider. It does sound fairly revolting but it emphasises the importance of attention to detail when caring for tarantulas.

Feeding. This is a fairly easy task, given that tarantulas will take only live food. Like many keepers, I feed my collection almost exclusively upon house crickets; indeed, some of my spiders will eat

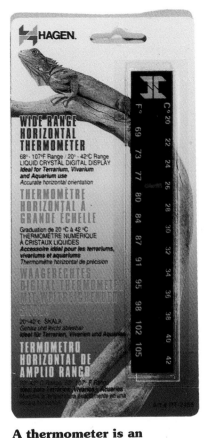

A thermometer is an inexpensive tool to obtain and is invaluable. Thermometers are useful for monitoring the temperature in your pet's terrarium. Photo courtesy of Hagen.

nothing else.

However, variety is the spice of life and alternatives can be offered such as African field crickets, locusts, mealworms,

Above: **Tarantulas feed on live food like this adult beetle.**

Below: **You may wish to spice up your tarantula's diet occasionally with locusts or insects other than crickets.**

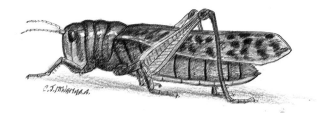

cockroaches, phasmids, large moths and even a pinkie mouse or hatchling chick for larger species. Most of the aforementioned are available commercially from pet stores and dealers, particularly those who deal in reptiles and amphibians. If you have just one spider, then clearly the best method is to buy food as you need it. However, we have found that caring for a large collection means breeding your own live food from both economy and availability aspects.

Many 'don'ts' in one place. Don't use gravel. Don't make the tank too large. Don't bother designing or decorating. Don't use a normal light hood unless you make it safe *and* escape-proof.

Most adult tarantulas require feeding only once a week and normally will accept two to three crickets at a session. If the offering

Lunch time! This tarantula feeds on its prey.

is ignored we leave the spider alone until next feeding day. If, however, the prey is instantly snared we drop in a further two insects. Spider appetites are very hard to gauge. Their intake of food depends on their general health, whether they are carrying eggs, and whether they are due to shed their skins. However, tarantulas can go for a year or more without food so one should never panic if the appetite appears non-existent for a few weeks or even months.

Rearing Spiderlings

Having covered adult, subadult and juveniles in the previous chapters, we now turn our attention to the mini-beast of the spider world, the spiderling. There is nothing more rewarding than watching this miniature tarantula begin to feed, moult, feed and moult again, but to bring up a baby tarantula needs a great deal more attention to detail than does its adult counterparts. This is certainly a more complicated, more time-consuming, aspect of the tarantula keeper's life.

Let us firstly cover spiderlings hatched from an egg sac laid by your own pet spider. What happens when your female tarantula lays what, to all intents and purposes, is a ball of cotton wool? If an arranged mating has not preceded this event, then obviously you will be somewhat surprised! The reason is either that she has been wild-collected and is in a gravid state, or it is a phantom pregnancy. In either event, the cotton wool ball is an egg sac! If this is fertile (if it is not she will eventually destroy it), depending upon species, in three to sixteen weeks you will have a hatching of miniature tarantulas looking nothing whatsoever like 'mum', sometimes emerging from the egg sac as tiny opaque-white eggs with legs, in quantities of 70-700! What to do with them?

The first thing you must do is remove the adult female, for if you do not she will undoubt-edly begin to eat the babies. While she is caring for the egg sac, you have plenty of time to prepare for her post-natal care by providing her with a new home. Once she has been removed and rehoused, you can worry about the spiderlings.

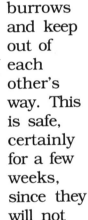

I have found the best method is to cram the tank half-way full with sphagnum moss and leave the spiderlings together. They will dig themselves tiny burrows and keep out of each other's way. This is safe, certainly for a few weeks, since they will not begin feeding immediately. Spiderlings have their first moult within the confines of the egg sac; they then emerge and a week or so later have their first moult outside the egg sac. At this

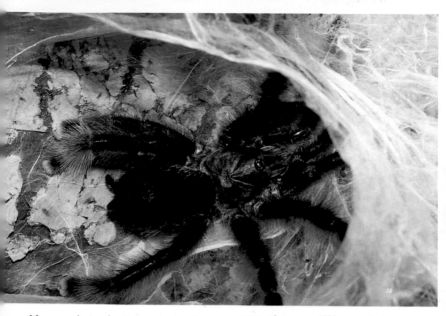

Above: Avicularia avicularia, South American Pink Toe Tarantula.

Opposite page: Brachypelma smithi, Mexican Red Knee Tarantula.

point they will need to be fed. Micro-crickets (hatchlings) and fruit flies *(Drosophila)* are ideal as spiderling food and are easily obtained via mail order. Provided you keep a constant supply of food and humid conditions, the spiderlings will co-habit for some few weeks more. By giving them

Front view of *Brachypelma smithi*, Mexican Red Knee Tarantula.

moss in addition to the normal tank substrate, they are perfectly happy.

Additional heating is not always necessary. For example, I have just recently reared a brood of 445 Mexican Red Rump/Black Velvet (*Brachypelma vagans*) spiderlings at room temperature (70°-75° F). In some cases you may need to increase temperatures (see individual descriptions).

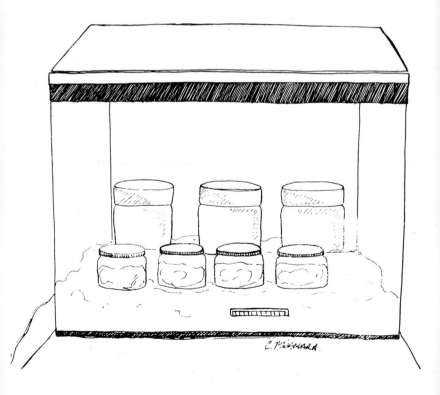

Above: **The "painted" appearance of this Indian Ornamental Black and White Tarantula,** *Poecilotheria regalis,* **is quite dramatic.**

Opposite page: **Recommended materials for spiderling housing.**

After four or five weeks, you will find that the spiderlings will require separating into individual containers. This is usually a fairly easy, if time-consuming task! However, it will have to be done.

The best containers are 60ml (about 2

ounces) plastic tubs that are available commercially. These tubs are also suitable for rearing spiderlings that you acquire from other breeders. You can utilise baby food jars or mini-yogurt jars provided they can be kept humid and warm.

Fill each tub one-third of its depth with damp vermiculite, add a small piece of sphagnum moss or snake grass, and pop in the baby spider. We have found the easiest way to catch the spiderlings without causing them injury is with a plastic specimen phial into which the spiderling can be driven with the finger tip.

Provided the humidity is high, but not so high as to drown the baby spider, you will not need to provide a water dish. However, a tiny ball of cotton wool or paper towel well soaked with fresh water and changed daily will not come amiss. Feeding should continue on a twice-a-week basis.

There are two methods of providing extra heat for spiderlings when needed, both of which I have used successfully:

1) A large polystyrene box with a lid which needs no other heating. The tubs are placed inside and

This beautiful baby is a spiderling of the Mexican Red Knee, *Brachypelma smithi*.

even, when necessary, piled on top of each other. This is also handy for transporting spiderlings by car.

2) A large fish tank or vivarium with a heating pad INSIDE and standing on end at the rear. The tubs can be stacked near but not touching the heating pad and stay warm and humid.

Of course, as the spiderlings grow you will need to move them into larger containers. From the 60ml tubs my spiderlings are moved on to a small glass tank 9" x 4-1/2" x 4-1/2" tall, divided into two, thereby giving each spiderling 4-1/2" x 4-1/2" ground space and enough growing room for a considerable length of time. Growth rate varies quite considerably between species (see individual descriptions).

MOULTING

This is, probably, the most traumatic time in the life of a tarantula, although spiderlings appear to cope far more easily, perhaps because they are moulting more frequently than their parents. A full-grown adult female usually moults annually, but there are notable exceptions to this rule, including one Mexican True Red Leg (*Brachypelma emilia*) that did not moult for over two years and several other examples of lengthy periods between moults.

Brachypelma emilia, more commonly known as the Mexican True Red Leg Tarantula.

Above: Often the loss of hairs on the abdomen indicates an approaching moult. *Opposite page:* If you must handle your tarantula, be sure to give it much more security.

Spiders need to shed their skins to enable them to grow. Even true spiders, i.e., the common British house spider (*Tegenaria* sp.), moult regularly

ten it is purely the cast skin of the web's owner.

The process of moulting can take anything from a few minutes for a spiderling

throughout their relatively short lives. Look in any spider web and you will often see what appears to be a dead spider hanging there; nine times out of

This little tarantula with the bumble-bee bottom is an adult male Tiger Rump Doppelganger, *Cylcosternum fasciata*.

The metallic gold look to the carapace gives this spider its common name Texas Big Bend Gold Carapace, *Eurypelma caniceps.*

to 24 hours for an adult. The majority of tarantulas moult in an average time of about three hours. Most of the ground-dwellers moult on their backs; arboreal spiders usually moult in their tube webs. However, it is not unheard of for the moult to take place with the spider standing on all eight legs! Whichever should be the case, the spider knows best; never touch or disturb a tarantula that is moulting; equally do not touch the spider for several days after the moult while it is still soft and prone to damage.

When you see your spider preparing for the moult, make sure all live food is removed from the tank since crickets and locusts, etc., can damage a moulting spider. Offer food again only four or five days following the casting of the skin, although spiderlings will often feed immediately following the moult.

A sign of the approach of the moult is primarily lack of appetite, some adult spiders ceasing to feed weeks or even months before. Ground-dwelling or burrowing spiders will almost always lay a thin mat of silk on the base of their tank and then flip over onto their back. Once the tarantula is free of its old skin (exoskeleton) it is tossed away. The spider remains upon its back, often for several hours (this is the time in the wild when spiders can be snatched away by predators, such as large birds, lizards, etc.), before flipping back onto its feet. The spider then flattens itself to the ground in a stretching pose and will stay like that sometimes for 24 hours before beginning to behave normally.

Contrary to popular belief, the bald patch that appears on the abdomen of several species, e.g., the Mexican Red Knee (*Brachypelma smithi*) and the Honduras Curly Hair

Brachypelma albopilosa, more commonly known as Honduras Curly Hair Tarantula.

A curly hair tarantula
dining on a cricket.

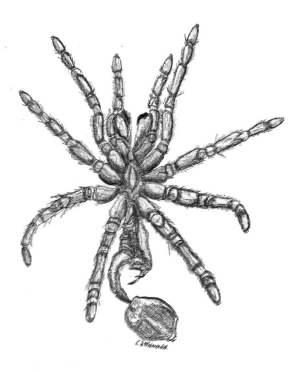

Above is an artist's rendering of a tarantula's moulted skin.

(*Brachypelma albopilosa*), is not necessarily a sign of an aging or dying spider. In some cases, particularly males, this may be true, but usually it is merely a sign of pre-moult. At the point when moulting is imminent, the patch will turn a definite blue-black. This patch is the spot where the abdomen skin splits to enable the tarantula to clamber out of its old skin.

Once the spider has moulted successfully, it appears you have two spiders in the tank so perfect is the cast skin. Many people do, in fact, set and mount the skins for display purposes. This can easily be done provided the skin is still damp and supple. You require a suitable container, i.e., a plastic cricket punnet (a small basket). Lay out the moulted skin in the required pose and stretch the abdomen skin around to a more natural position. Fill out the abdomen skin with cotton wool or kitchen tissue and tack into position with a small drop of wood glue. The carapace cover can also be reattached in this way and, if you wish, you can touch each toe underneath with the glue so that the skin remains in place in the punnet. This can make a very attractive display, especially with the larger and more

colourful spiders. Bear in mind that the skins do dry out very rapidly, which makes them brittle. In later stages of this book you will read of an even more important use for the moulted skin. My good friend and colleague, John Hancock, has used them to produce some data on sexing tarantulas that prove

Above: **A tarantula with its moulted skin.**

Opposite page: **A wolf spider with cottonball-like sac of eggs.**

vital when planning a captive breeding programme.

Often your spider will, for one reason or another, cast a limb. The usual reason for this is a break, the broken leg being discarded as of no further use! One of the amazing things about spiders is that they have the ability to regenerate the lost appendage; this strange phenomenon takes place in the next moult. The new limb, although perfectly formed, is often slightly slimmer and perhaps not so colourful as the other seven. If you watch closely after each successive moult, you will find the leg becoming stronger and stronger until, eventually, there is no difference between the new one and other appendages. I have a South American Pink Toe (*Avicularia avicularia*) that came to me minus three legs and one pedipalp. I did not hold out much hope for her survival, but within three moults (she was juvenile at the time) she had become a perfect example of her species. Spiders are certainly amazing creatures.

Avicularia avicularia,
**South American Pink Toe
Tarantula.**

Dugesiella hentzi, the Texas Brown. This specimen is from Arkansas.

Pamphobeteus tetracanthus from Brazil, one of the bird-eaters.

Scientific Names

Though considered a source of much confusion, in reality the scientific name often is neither so confusing nor hard to remember as is the common name! For example, what a mouthful is the Campina Grande Salmon Pink Bird Eater! Or how about the Tiger Rump Doppelganger? Worse still, the Mombasa Golden Starburst Baboon (this does, in fact, have eight legs, not just four, and isn't in the least ape-like!). Having said that, some of the scientific names tell us little or nothing about the spider either. Take the Mexican Red Knee (*Brachypelma smithi*). All this scientific name tells us is that this is a *Brachypelma* (now *Euathlus*) spider species probably first discovered by a Mr. Smith! It certainly, in translation, tells us nothing about the colouration of this particular beast. I am certainly no Latin scholar so I am not about to pontificate on the meanings of certain of the scientific (Latin) names of tarantula species, but it does serve to

You do not have to know the scientific name of your tarantula, but it helps.

illustrate the confusion that can abound.

Then we come to pet store confusion! The prime example of this is the great Chilean debate: the Chilean Rose or Rosy ! There are two species lumped together under this pet store name—the Chilean Beautiful Tarantula (*Grammostola cala*) and

Grammostola actaeon **from South America. This is a far-southern relative of the familiar Mexican Red Leg Tarantula.**

Brachypelma smithi, a Mexican Red Knee Tarantula.

the Chilean Common Tarantula (*Grammostola spatulata*). Just to make matters worse yet, along came a totally different species, the Chilean Yellow Rump (*Phryxotrichus auratus*), giving further problems when sold under the 'Chilean Rose' handle. One cannot really blame the storekeeper, for often he doesn't know the names of the spiders he offers for sale. He can use only the name given to him by the wholesaler or importer, and if they have it wrong from the source of supply, then it becomes a vicious circle serving only to make life more difficult

Opposite page: A male
Grammostola burzaquensis
from Argentina.

*Above: Grammostola
spatulata,* a Chilean Common
Tarantula.

for pet owners and a nightmare for breeders! The confusion was further accentuated when two species were totally different but looked much the same at first glance. These were relatively small species, the Costa Rican Sun Tiger Abdomen (*Metriopelma zebrata*), and the Tiger Rump Doppelganger (*Cyclosternum fasciata*). Oh, my word, did it get complicated! Both species have survived in captivity and are now easily distinguished one from the other, but at the time it made life very difficult.

Then we come to the problem of worldwide common names. They simply, in many cases, do not exist! In the U.S.A., *Brachypelma smithi* is known as the Mexican Red Leg; in the U.K. this is the Mexican Red Knee! Then we have *Brachypelma emilia*. In the U.S.A. this is the Painted Tarantula, the Red Banded Tarantula and the Red Legged Tarantula; in the U.K. this is the Mexican True Red Leg! It gets worse! Along comes *Brachypelma mesomelas*. Again, in the U.S.A. they are often referred to as the Red Legged Tarantula, the Orange Kneed Tarantula and probably many more names; in the U.K. this is the Costa Rican Red Leg! About the only spider upon which the

Theraphosa leblondi, a Goliath Bird Eater.

world agrees regarding common names is *Theraphosa leblondi* (the Goliath Bird Eater) and who, I wonder, can top that! I rest my case!

Naturally, everyone knows that the genus is the first part of a scientific name (let's call it the surname) and begins with an upper case letter; the second name is always written with a lower case initial; i.e.,

Grammostola cala. Why this is so is a mystery to me, but then as I have mentioned I am no Latin scholar! For the purposes of this book I have compiled a list of 38 species of tarantula (individually described in the second part), quoting their common names and their scientific names as follows:

1. Bolivian Steely-Blue Legged Bird Eater—*Pamphobeteus antinious*

Brachypelma smithi, Mexican Red Leg Tarantula.

A giant Colombian tarantula, *Pamphobeteus* sp.

2. Campina Grande Salmon Pink Bird Eater—*Lasiodora parahybana*

3. Chilean Beautiful Tarantula—*Grammostola cala*

4. Chilean Common Tarantula—*Grammostola spatulata*

5. Chilean Yellow Rump—*Phryxotrichus auratus*

6. Cobalt (or Burmese) Blue—*Haplopelma lividus*

7. Colombian Giant Bird Eaters—*Acanthoscurria/ Xenethis* sp.

8. Colombian Purple Bloom Bird Eater—*Pamphobeteus insignis*

9. Common Orange Rump—*Citharacanthus longipes*

10. Costa Rican Blue Front—*Citharacanthus crinirufus*

11. Costa Rican Red Leg—*Brachypelma mesomelas*

12. Costa Rican Sun Tiger Abdomen—*Metriopelma zebrata*

13. Costa Rican Zebra—*Aphonopelma seemanni*

14. East African Horned Baboon—*Ceratogyrus darlingi*

15. Entre Rios Tarantula—*Grammostola iheringi*

16. Goliath Bird Eater—*Theraphosa leblondi*

17. Haitian Brown—*Phormictopus cancerides*

18. Honduras Curly Hair—*Brachypelma albopilosa*

19. Indian Ornamental Black and White—*Poecilotheria regalis*

20. Mergui Reddish

Phoneutria sp., South American Wandering Spider.

Brown—*Ornithoctonus andersonni*

21. Mexican Black Velvet/Red Rump—*Brachypelma vagans*

22. Mexican Blonde/Palomino—*Aphonopelma chalcodes*

23. Mexican Red Knee—*Brachypelma smithi*

24. Mexican True Red Leg—*Brachypelma emilia*

25. Mombasa Golden Starburst Baboon—*Pterinochilus murinus*

26. Pampas Tawny Red—*Grammostola pulchripes*

27. Singapore Reddish Brown—

Opposite page: Brachypelma vagans, Mexican Red Rump/ Black Velvet Tarantula.

Above: Note the stripes and the prolific web of this Thailand Black Tarantula, *Melopoeus/Haplopelma minax.*

Coremiocnemis validus

28. South American Horned Baboon— *Spaerobothria hoffmanni*

29. South American Pink Toe—*Avicularia avicularia*

30. South American Yellow Banded— *Avicularia variegata/ magdalena*

31. Texas Big Bend Gold Carapace— *Eurypelma caniceps*

32. Texas Brown— *Dugesiella hentzi*

33. Thailand Black— *Haplopelma minax*

34. Tiger Rump Doppelganger— *Cyclosternum fasciata*

35. Trinidad Chevron—*Psalmopoeus cambridgei*

36. Trinidad Mahogany Brown— *Tapenauchenius plumipes*

37. Trinidad Olive Brown Spider— *Hapalopus incei*

38. White Collared— *Pterinopelma saltator*

In reality, the average pet keeper would not necessarily need to know the scientific name of his pet spider. However, once you come into contact with other like-minded arachnophiles (spider lovers!) it can be extremely useful to have some small amount of knowledge. Equally, identifying your tarantula if the pet store name is wrong can usually only

Poecilotheria regalis, **Indian Ornamental Black and White Tarantula.**

be done by tracking down the scientific name.

Some of the generic names quoted in the list will change, or have already changed in the scientific papers of some experts, as new information is published. Many, for example, of the '*Brachypelma*' species will become '*Euathlus*', and some of the '*Aphonopelma*' species are now '*Rhechostica*' according to some specialists. Confused? I am!!

PET NAMES?

Now that we have, in some small way, sorted out the problems of names, what do we do about pet names for tarantulas? Do we or do we not give them

names and, if we do, what criteria do we adopt for selecting the name?

The scientific-minded will inevitably say that pet names are not necessary and really rather silly and inappropriate. After all, the tarantula, as far as is known, has no hearing ability, so what is the point? Those who keep tarantulas for study and research no doubt use a numbering system, as do those with large hatchings of spiderlings. I, however,

Aphonopelma seemanni,
**Costa Rican Zebra
Tarantula.**

am one who gives all my animals names (and the sillier the better!), from 'Wally' the cockatiel to 'Nikki' the cross-bred Irish Setter. So why not the spiders too?

Choice, if you consider it carefully, is fairly vast. My friends Dennis and Carol give their spiders names which reflect their own roots in Wales. The spiders are called 'Bronwyn', 'Blodwyn', 'Megan', 'Bethany', etc. Christine McNamara (whose marvellous illustrations are contained in this book) gives her spiders names, sometimes, that go with their common names, i.e., 'Rosey' is a Chilean Rose. There are those among us who go to the other extreme with reflective names, like 'Fang', 'Biter', 'Dracula', 'Boris', etc. My first pet tarantula was 'Stripey' (a Mexican Red Knee offered the name by my mother) and I then called two more spiders after my parents, 'Victoria' and 'Albert'.

Now that the

ATTILA

Pet tarantulas need pet names! Your imagination is your only limit.

collection has grown, we are running out of ideas so we have gone to another extreme, giving the later additions names that do not in any way reflect what they are; our *Theraphosa* *leblondi* is now known as 'Buttercup'!! As aforesaid, names for me are the sillier the better!!

There is absolutely no reason that I can accept for not giving a pet spider a pet name!

Avicularia avicularia, South American Pink Toe Tarantula.

Handling Spiders

If you have to handle your spider, then do so with great care, keeping in mind that the spider you have is a wild animal; it is also a delicate creature who can be caused serious, even fatal, damage if dropped; it is *NOT* handled in the wild.

The tarantula's abdomen is very soft and vulnerable; it can split like a paper bag filled with jelly if it falls from even just a few inches, and there is no way of repairing such damage.

Never grasp a tarantula in such a way that its abdomen is in danger of being squeezed...and never hold a tarantula in a way that puts it in danger of being dropped. Picking the tarantula up the way shown here (that is, from above) is the wrong way.

A Curly
HairTarantula.

Never, never pick up a spider from above, e.g., with your fingers between the four pairs of legs. This method is widely used by scientists, but you need to be very sure of what you are doing. It is only too easy to crush this delicate creature internally if you apply even the slightest pressure. I have, in fact, known this to happen when a young lad of my acquaintance actually killed two of his spiders in this way and was utterly devastated.

I cannot be too dogmatic about not handling tarantulas since this would be hypocritical. All I can do is to stress that great care should be taken and, further,

that handling spiders should not be for the pleasure of the handler. It is dangerous practice and should be avoided if at all possible.

I have three spiders that are, for want of a better word, handleable: (1) Cleo (Mexican Red Knee); (2) Jemima (White Collared) and (3) Albert (Honduras Curly Hair). The method I always employ is to approach the tarantula from the rear and gently stroke the abdomen with one finger, when normally any of the three will remain stationary. I then place my other hand flat in front of the animal, who usually will walk forward using the hand as substrate.

Tarantulas should be handled with care, if at all. Most will bite, and all are unpredictable.

She/he can then be gently lifted out of the tank for whatever reason. Cleo, Jemima and Albert all normally react nicely to being handled and are usually docile. However, I am constantly aware that they are wild creatures with all the natural instincts of hunters. I have only to watch them snare their prey to have this point brought firmly home!

When it comes to handling 99% of the tarantulas listed earlier, fingers and/or human hands are vulnerable. The best method yet devised for moving a large, aggressive spider from tank to tank is an idea first used by my friend Vince Hull-Williams.

Take an empty two-litre plastic lemonade bottle and cut it in half, discarding the bottom half. Place the half with the screw top over the spider, who will usually climb upward. A piece of card slid under the half bottle makes it an easy matter to lift the spider into a new home. It certainly works.

An escapee tarantula can usually be recaptured by dropping the same bottle over the spider, sliding a piece of card between

Although none of the tarantulas kept as pets are dangerous, all have large fangs capable of inflicting deep bites. All also have a mild venom.

spider and the surface upon which it is standing and lifting.

Spiders are great 'Houdini s'—if they can get their two front walking legs and pedipalps through a gap, somehow they manage to get the rest of their body through. Therefore, make certain your spider tank has a *very* secure lid!

If you do have an escapee that cannot be located, think about it before you panic! Ground-dwellers almost always migrate downward into dark corners, inside cupboards and even shoes, anywhere it is warm and dark. Arboreal spiders almost always head up! Ceiling corners, on top of cupboards. Remembering the small space syndrome, holes in skirting boards make it easy for an escapee to avoid detection.

The worst thing you can do if you find your tarantula has packed up and left home is to fret. Ninety-nine percent of the time the spider returns. One I heard of reappeared exactly a year after it left and to this day is safe and well. The lesson was well learned and it has not escaped since.

Because their soft abdomens burst easily if dropped, never give your pet a 'ride' on your hand without supporting it.

Tarantulas and The Vet

Normally spiders do not need the services of a vet! Many of this proud profession will be relieved to know that. I know my vet is very pleased not to have to treat my spiders!

The focal 'medical' problems that can befall tarantulas are *falls*, *moulting* and *parasites*. Since, as far as is known, tarantulas carry no form of disease that can be communicated to humans or domestic livestock, it is as well to know what to do if any of the above-mentioned problems occur. Some can be cured; some have unfortunately to be endured.

FALLS—Be they arboreal or terrestrial, spiders almost always climb the sides of their tanks now and again and they can, of course, fall. If the tank is a maximum of 8"-12" high, then harm is unlikely to beset them unless the fall culminates upon a piece of bark, stone or plant matter (ergo, *NEVER* use cacti, or stones and gravel and keep bark away from the edges). A handled

A tarantula's abdomen is its weakest point. A leg may be regenerated, but a burst abdomen means death.

spider or one in an over-tall tank is the more vulnerable. With luck, a fall will simply cause a jarred or sprained limb, but in some cases the limb can be broken, often resulting in bleeding at the joints. The blood of the tarantula is a colourless fluid but is clearly visible seeping from a damaged joint. The bleeding must be stopped and there is a very simple method of doing this. Plain talcum powder (unperfumed) or icing sugar (YES! icing sugar!) dusted lightly over the affected area stems the blood flow. Vaseline is another coagulant but is harder to apply to a less than docile spider. If either of these methods is employed as soon as the injury is discovered, then all will be well. Do *NOT* however overdo the icing sugar, since if sprinkled too heavily once the injury is healed the humidity in the tank leaves the spider with the appearance of a walking iced-bun! Although this does not harm the spider, he or she being merely rather sticky, it does detract slightly from the creature's beauty. The icing can be removed by gently rolling it up around a cotton bud but it is obviously preferable not to get into that position in the first place. My friend, Sue Clarke, invented this method when she was

How *not* to handle your tarantula! This specimen could easily bite if annoyed or surprised, and its stinging hairs are sure to get into the skin of the hand that is holding it.

faced with an urgent problem of bleeding and had nothing else available.

In severe cases, for example when the skeleton is broken or badly damaged, the spider will cast the leg to be regenerated in future moults. On occasions the cast leg is actually eaten by the spider; sometimes food insects will nibble a cast leg.

A split abdomen is far more serious. Often

the tarantula owner will be unaware there is a problem and the spider can literally bleed to death. If, however, an injury is spotted, a small split can be treated as mentioned above. A really severe split is unfortunately incurable and the kindest thing to do is to put the spider out of its misery by placing it in the freezer.

MOULTING—This is the time when, in the wild, the tarantula is at its most vulnerable. A time when predators, such as large birds, lizards, etc., will snatch the spider away as a tasty lunch. In captivity it is no less traumatic but is relatively safe and it is rare for a tarantula to die during or immediately following the moult. Reasons for moult death are usually (i) an old spider who simply has not the strength to survive; (ii) lack of humidity—always keep the tank well sprayed during pre-moult; (iii) haemorrhage, which is almost impossible to detect and even if noticed is unlikely to be curable; (iv) a moult too quickly following upon a previous moult, meaning that

The bloody trail left by this tarantula indicates a possibly fatal accident has occurred. Terminal specimens may be euthanised in the freezer.

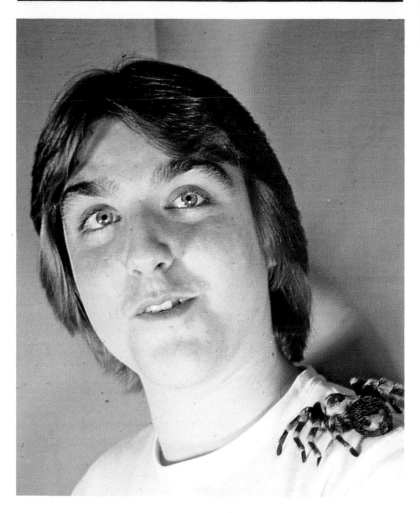

An accident waiting to happen. Please be careful at all times with your pet.

the endoskeleton has not grown sufficiently to allow another moult; (v) lack of knowledge on the owner's part. Witness the inexperienced keeper finding a pet tarantula on its back. The first instinct is to turn the spider back onto its feet, which can be *fatal*!

PARASITES—A parasitised spider is a pathetic sight to behold and it is sad to say there is nothing to be done for a spider so infested. The usual cause is a wasp (the Tarantula Hawk) that lays its eggs under the abdominal skin of the spider. The egg lies dormant for long periods and is undetectable until the grub hatches. The

The Tarantula Hawk Wasp.

spider host, in fact, often looks perfectly normal to start with. The wasp stings the spider first to anesthetise it while she does her deadly work. Once the grub hatches, it literally feeds on the spider's

Above: Pterinochilus murinus, Mombasa Golden Starburst Baboon Tarantula.

Opposite page: Pterinopelma saltator, White Collared Tarantula.

living tissue until it emerges through the abdomen skin and flies away. Apart from a possible slightly misshapen abdomen, other signs of parasitic prescence are a tendency on the spider's part to over-preen or scratch; the spider will be restless and obviously unhappy. There is no treatment and the spider will inevitably die. Until these parasitic grubs begin hatching, it is impossible to know the spider is parasitised and by then it is too

late. Realistically this can only happen with wild-collected specimens. Captive bred is a far safer way of obtaining stock and of prolonging many species of tarantula, some of which are all but on the verge of extinction; many more are endangered.

LIFE SPANS

If you treat your tarantula with care, it will be with you for many years, the females generally living the longest. Some Mexican Red Knee females can live up to 30 years. The average is around 12 to 14 years, therefore roughly the same as a dog or cat.

It is worth mentioning here the differences between a mature male and a mature female. Adults, depending upon species, mature between 18 months and five years of age. Many people do not keep records of their spider's moulting cycle, and unless you have had the spider from hatching, it is very hard to assess accurately its age. It has to be said that the maturation span mentioned above does vary between the species and even between individuals of the same species.

Until recently it has been impossible to be sure, when you first acquire your tarantula, whether you have a male or a female. It is a proven fact that in some cases even the spiders themselves are unsure of their gender (see individual description—Haitian Brown). However, work currently being done is going to make ascertaining the sex of the tarantula much easier. In a later chapter my colleague, John Hancock, writes on this subject.

Referring back to the differences between the genders, a mature male will have grown, in most cases, two visible hooks or spurs on the tibias of his front pair of walking legs. His pedipalps will have become bulbous like miniature boxing gloves. His abdomen will be considerably smaller than the female counterpart and his legs are usually longer and more 'spindly or leggy' in appearance.

At this time he will be extremely active and will parade about his tank. Once he has built his sperm web he will be simply seeking a mate. Males live, on average, from nine to 16 months after a maturing moult and their sole purpose is to mate with as many females as possible. The male spider generally has his days numbered once he matures.

Talking of dying spiders is a sad though natural fact, and a few pointers may be helpful. A dead tarantula is invariably found in a 'scrunched-

External anatomy of a tarantula: 1. cephalothorax; 2. abdomen; 3. apodeme; 4. spinnerets; 5. anus; 6. eyes; 7. chelicera; 8. carapace; 9. pedipalp.

Phidippus **sp., Texas Jumping Spider.**

up' position with legs tucked underneath. This happens some days before actual death. The brain is the first organ that ceases to function, but the central nervous system remains alive for a few days more. This can clearly be seen by touching a rear leg gently, when definite although extremely slow movement can be observed. When this movement is no longer noted, then it can be safely assumed that the spider has expired. There is no evidence to suggest that the creature is in any pain and therefore he should be allowed the dignity of dying naturally. If, at any time, distress is noticed then the kindest thing for him is to place him in the freezer, where death will be rapid.

VENOMOUS SPIDERS

All spiders, even the tiny Money Spider, are venomous to varying degrees, but there is much research currently being undertaken to ascertain exactly how much venom and what type of venom spiders have. To date, the theraphosids (the tarantulas) are considered as among the least dangerous of the spiders in the world. A bite would be no worse than that of a bee or wasp. Therefore, those who are allergic to such stings should, obviously, avoid contact with a tarantula to eliminate the risk. For a healthy adult, there would be no problems ensuing from a tarantula bite, but with fangs the size that they are, a bite would no doubt prove painful. I have never been bitten, nor have I given the spiders the chance to bite me, but accidents do happen and even the most careful arachnologist can fall prey to a nip occasionally. As far as is known currently, no one has ever been killed from a bite of any of the tarantulas kept in captivity, but research is always continuing.

The theory that I hold dear is that should a tarantula inflict a bite upon a human hand, the spider instantly realises that this is not edible and therefore does not waste her precious venom on something she cannot consume. Thus the amount of venom injected through the fangs would be minimal.

The lethal spiders consist mainly of such as the Black Widow (*Latrodectus mactans*), the Red Back (*Latrodectus hasselti*) and the Funnel Web (*Atrax* sp.), all of which are considered dangerous and, of course, do not make good pets.

Having mentioned toxicity, it should be noted that the hairs from some of the tarantulas are considered toxic, again in varying degrees, and can cause rashes and other unpleasant symptoms. Some tarantulas are noted 'hair kickers'; that is to say, they scratch their abdomens vigourously with a rear leg, usually in defence, and send clouds of ultra-fine hairs into the surrounding atmosphere. These are the hairs that have caused problems on occasion. It has been

Opposite page: The hairiness of a tarantula's body and legs is well illustrated in this view of a tarantula's underside. Some hairs serve as sensory instruments, and some are used in defensive maneuvers.

Below: An *Acanthoscurria* species from Argentina.

proven that some people are allergic to these hairs.

Research into these urticating hairs is once again constantly being carried out and the many stories that are forthcoming regarding the effects of contact with these hairs are being thoroughly studied. When the

hairs are sent in clouds into the atmosphere, it has been reported that eyes and nasal passages become irritated and even inflamed when hairs connect.

It is even thought possible that the hairs have a cumulative effect (John Nichol 1986) and one report tells that following a hair kicking session by a Mexican Red Knee (one of the main culprits) an 'itch' was noticed on the hand. On viewing the affected area under strong light the hairs could clearly be seen, not singly, but in clumps. If these were removed with tweezers fairly quickly the discomfort would not last long. Left to their own devices the irritation would continue and worsen. Mexican Red Knee hairs are the cause of most of the problems. After changing water in the tanks, one report tells that a rash appeared on the forearms and even across the lower chest of the keeper. This irritated for several days before disappearing but tends to return from time to time (Dennis Toulson 1988), thus bearing out the cumulative effect theory.

The South American Pink Toe is another tarantula whose hairs have been known to affect the forearms by way of a nettlerash-like infection, but with red bumps instead of white. The areas affected were extremely sore and the effect lasted about a week. The same person found that the hairs had inched into the eye. After several rubbings and washings, the tearduct and the skin surrounding the eye (not the external lids but the flesh around the actual eyeball) had swollen. The eyeball, except for the pupil and iris, was covered with half a millimetre of thick opaque jelly. The accompanying irritation was comparable to conjunctivitis, but with regular washes in cold water the irritation and the jelly disappeared within three hours (Mike Byron 1988).

I therefore stress once again that care and caution should abound when handling or dealing with tarantulas, especially those who are noted 'hair kickers'.

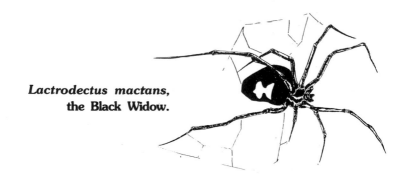

Lactrodectus mactans,
the Black Widow.

Opposite page: **A Black Widow Spider with egg case.**

Above: ***Mastigoproctus giganteus*, the largest whipscorpion in the world.**

Cleo Meets the Media

There is nothing the newspapers like better than a spider story and they are, it has to be said, most inventive when it comes to reporting on the topic. The Mexican Red Knee comes in for the most horrific publicity at times.

My favourite spider, Cleo, has been around these people for many years now and has always, so far, behaved perfectly for them. She started her 'cover-girl' career with the local newspapers, progressed to the Nationals and thence to the glossy magazines, having been spotted as far away as South Africa.

The thing about the Mexican Red Knee is its perfect suitability for colour or black and white photography. Cleo is also fairly large, which again lends weight to the huge, hairy spider theme.

She, and two of my other spiders, have become seasoned campaigners on both the British Radio and Television services. On a highly popular chat-show recently, Cleo played her part like a trooper, even allowing our host the dubious pleasure of stroking her. However, came the time to return to her tank (and she was only a few inches out of it) she decided she preferred the comfort of my velvet jacket to damp vermiculite. Eight legs clamped around my wrist and nothing would budge her. By the time the cameras had gone on to the next item, the table, complete with Cleo's tank, had been removed by stage hands and spider and self had no choice but to leave the stage with trepidation. A few minutes later she was persuaded to return to her box!

Albert, my Honduras Curly Hair (*Brachypelma albopilosa*) behaved in a less than gentlemanly manner on a radio chat-show. At the time, Albert was an immature male and had never shown any tendency toward escapology. However, I spoke the words that changed all that when explaining that he would not climb out if the lid were removed from his tank. Clearly Albert did not understand plain English and proceeded out of his tank and across the desk to the great delight of our host, who described to the listening public just what was happening. Fortunately, this particular host is a spider lover, but Albert certainly gave us a few hairy moments on live radio.

When recording a programme for Granada Television, Jemima, my White Collared (*Pterinopelma*

A gorgeous specimen of the Mexican Red
Leg Tarantula, *Brachypelma smithi,* the
species favored by many keepers.

saltator), was the perfect little lady, performing beautifully and returning to her box on cue. The director then informed us that they had not taken the correct shot of her and would we do it all again!

The media is wonderful!

Talks and lectures are always good fun and of course a vital course of good publicity for arachnology. There are, occasionally, hairy moments in giving these talks. Explaining to a group of schoolboys aged between 11 and 18 about the Mexican Red Knee, Cleo suddenly took it into her head to run. This she did up my arm and lodged herself in my hair! I knew where she was from the weight but I could not see her and resorted to placing my hand completely over her. As luck would have it she ran back down my arm and into her tank once more. That of course could have been dangerous for her since had she fallen she would not be alive today. The only thing I can think of which made her behave so out of character was that one of the boys breathed on her. Tarantulas are very susceptible to wafts of air.

One question that comes up again and again when talking to the media or to groups of students is, what do tarantulas do?

Basically, the simple answer to that is, not very much. They are very quiet peaceful creatures and, of course, are nocturnal in habit, which means they rest during the day. At night it can be a very different story for it is then they are at their most active. It is this time in a 24-hour cycle that the tarantula will re-landscape its home, upset its water dish and generally wreak havoc upon the custom-designed tank you have lovingly prepared for it.

The age-old phrase 'never work with children or animals' goes double for tarantulas who are so unpredictable that they will either steal the show or retreat into a corner and show not one single hair.

THE SPIDER AND ITS WEBS

Spider webs are diagnostic; in other words, one can usually tell the identity of the owner by the type of web construction. This is perfectly obvious in true spiders like the common British garden spider and equally so with tarantulas. Most of the ground-dwellers from the New World lay fine mats of silk rather than actual circular constructions. However, touch the substrate of a ground-dwelling tarantula after she has been in residence for a week or so and you will often find she has 'welded'

Tapenauchenius plumipes, Trinidad Mahogany Brown Tarantula.

the substrate together with silk.

New World arboreal spiders weave webs that are far more obvious. Many of the Old World ground-dwellers spin prolifically around and inside their burrow, lining the sides and the roof with thick silk. The South American Pink Toes (*Avicularia avicularia*) spin tube-like constructions so thick that it is impossible to tear with the bare hands. They not only live but also moult, feed and lay their egg sacs within these hardy constructions. They do their 'housework' by turning out various pieces of flotsam and jetsam no longer required and, if the web becomes too dirty, they will either destroy and rebuild on the same site or move further along and construct a new nest.

The Trinidad Chevron Tree Spider (*Psalmopoeus cambridgei*) also builds webs in trees in the wild, but in captivity I have found that these spiders frequently build their tubular webs lower down in their container, sometimes even upon the ground. The Mombasa Golden Starburst Baboon Spider (supposedly a ground-dweller—at least according to all data on record) has been noted in captivity to select a corner of its tank, at the top, and

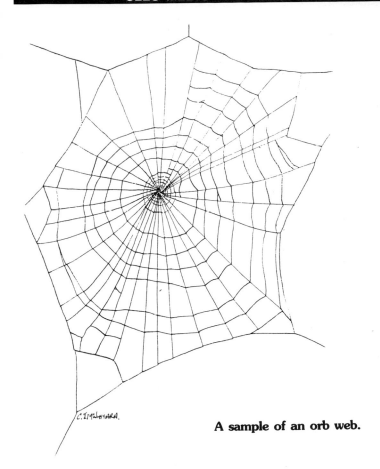

A sample of an orb web.

build a hammock-like construction wherein it lurks! Obviously it doesn't read the right books!

All spider webs are exceedingly strong and durable. The Giant Nephila spiders living in Africa and India can

Above: A South American Pink Toe (*Avicularia avicularia*) making her nest web.

Opposite page: A spider has cast its orb web in the mountains of Anjouan.

build webs up to 30 feet across, and often the remains of quite large birds are found. This is not to suggest that the spider catches the birds; normally the birds fly into the webs and become trapped in the sticky silk.

During the Roman invasion of Britain, the soldiers of Caesar's army used spider webs as bandages to bind two sides of a wound together. They did the job very well, but unfortunately the webs were full to bursting with bacteria, and the soldier usually died of an infection!

Spider webs are functional as well as very beautiful to the eye, and the spider will repair its web daily if necessary. There is nothing more fascinating than watching a spider spinning or catching prey.

Amongst other tarantulas that construct webs, consider the Trinidad Olive Brown Spider (*Hapalopus incei*) as highly proficient. The tunnels are dug through the substrate and the webs constructed with literally dozens of tunnels leading off and often out. The Cobalt Blue (*Haplopelma lividus*) and the Thailand Black (*Haplopelma minax*) also build tunnels once they have dug out a burrow and again the silk they spin is thick and incredibly strong. However, the king of the tarantulas as far as web building goes must be the Mergui Reddish Brown (*Ornithoctonus andersonni*). This large Old World tarantula from Burma is typical of its kind but its webs are something else. Within 24 hours of installation in a new tank it has webbed everywhere, even covering the surrounds to its water dish, but with some kind of super-spider intelligence it leaves a hole big enough for one to pour in top-up water. It is amazing. The web is extremely dense, and the spider literally lurks at the web entrance.

LONERS?

Tarantula spiders are in no way gregarious; in other words, they should never be housed with another unless in a divided tank. I am often posed the question of whether it is cruel to keep them singly and this I am definite about—it would be cruel to keep them together. At best they would fight; at worst they would kill one another. As previously mentioned, tarantulas do not need a lot of space and, in the wild, a female tarantula will make her burrow leaving it only occasionally to feed or drink. She will normally admit a male to her burrow for mating purposes, but

Opposite page: An orb-weaver spider.

Above: A Mergui Reddish Brown Tarantula, *Ornithoctonus andersonni*, lurks at a tunnel entrance.

once he has scurried away she will remain in her seemingly solitary and lonely state until she lays her egg sac. When the young emerge, she is not necessarily a good mother and the spiderlings, after their first moult outside the egg sac, will normally disperse to feed and find their own niches. Very few will survive in a wild environment, which is probably the reasoning for Nature allowing spiders to produce so many young.

Therefore, it is most definitely not cruel to house your captive tarantula on its own; in fact, it is essential.

Divided tanks are a good solution and can be extremely successful provided the divider is securely fitted, meeting the top of the tank and thus preventing either of the spiders from climbing into its neighbour's territory. I have had frantic telephone calls on this subject when one or other spiders has 'got in' with the inmate across the 'garden wall' and the spiders are fighting. There is only one answer to this problem and that is to separate them as quickly as possible. A sheet of strong cardboard and a plant atomiser spray are vital aids for this operation. If the card cannot be immediately inserted between them, a light spray from the atomiser will often part the fighting spiders sufficiently to allow the card to be slid into place and the marauder returned to its own home. However, it can be a serious problem and believe me, the spider can, *and will*, get through a very small space given the opportunity. If this happens once, it could be understood; twice is pure carelessness and three times borders upon lunacy. Safety for the tarantula and the keeper must be paramount on the list of importance.

It is possible to keep several spiderlings together once they have emerged from the egg sac, certainly for a week or so. If you fill the container with sphagnum moss, the spiderlings will delve into this, making their own little burrows and keeping out of their brothers' and sisters' way.

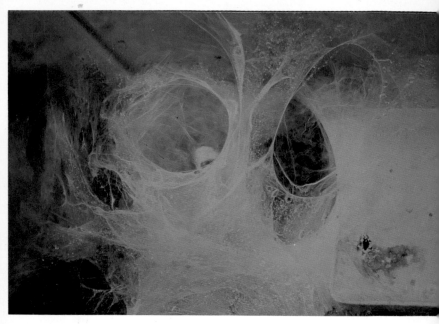

Above: Web of a Mergui
Reddish Brown Tarantula. Note
the 'webbed-in' water dish on
the left.

Opposite page: This spider,
Argiope aurantia, is a
common orb-weaver spider.

Captive Breeding-

It can be either if you let it! Pleasure is obviously the better alternative.

Many of the tarantulas we keep in captivity are either already endangered or could well be so in the not too distant future. It follows therefore that we must preserve what wild stocks remain in their natural habitat and if we want to continue to keep these beautiful beasts as pets, we must breed them. Intensive captive breeding programmes are being carried out in many U.K. zoos and animal establishments worldwide. Indeed the British Tarantula Society has its own highly successful breeding programme.

So what happens when a male matures in your collection and how do you know you have a male anyway? The chapters on anatomy and sexing theraphosids will give you vital points, but basically the male will have (in most species) grown tibial hooks on his two front walking legs, his pedipalps will have become bulbous like miniature boxing gloves, his abdomen will be much smaller and his legs will appear longer.

We now discuss what happens when you definitely have a male tarantula.

–Pain or Pleasure?

A week or so following the maturing moult the male will spin a small hammock-like web usually corner to corner of his container. He will then crawl on his back beneath this web (known as a sperm web) to deposit his sperm thereon. His next move is to clamber on top of the web and fill his two pedipalps with sperm. Having performed this ritual he will usually destroy the web and will either leave it bundled up in a corner or eat it. His hard work over, he will now be extremely active, charging about his tank and trying everything possible to escape.

The answer to his problem (yours too!) is to find someone with a female of the same species. Once this has been achieved, there are no further problems.

The best way to mate a pair of tarantulas is the tried and tested method. Make sure, firstly, that both are very well fed over a few days preceding the encounter. Early evening has proved to be the best time to achieve results with mating, so arm yourself with a plant atomiser spray and a piece of strong card in

Opposite page: **This species of spider, *Nephila clavipes*, is found only in the southeastern portions of the United States.**

Above: Pterinopelma saltator, **male White Collared Tarantula.**

case a disagreement springs up between male and female. I always have a pair of long tweezers at hand in addition to the above.

So the scene is set and the preparation made.

Place the male into the female's tank (*never* the other way around) and sit back to watch proceedings. Often, although not always, the male performs a kind of dance by drumming with his front feet and pedipalps upon the substrate; equally often if she is willing, the female responds by drumming back. The male quivers all over, dipping his abdomen up and down into the substrate. This performance over, the male will dash over, at which point the female will rear up exposing her fangs. It is the work of seconds for the male to hook onto her fangs with his tibial spurs and begin to inseminate her by slipping his pedipalps one by one and across into her genital openings. With her fangs engaged the male has no immediate worries that she will bite him, but once the mating is complete he must keep her pacified until he can break away. This he does by loosening one fang and using that leg to stroke the female's abdomen while he disengages his second hook. Once this is achieved he will run usually backward waving his pedipalps and two front walking legs in the air until, finally, he is far enough out of her reach to turn and be collected quickly to return to his own home. Pairings usually take around 10-30 seconds.

Usually, one mating between a pair is sufficient, but it does no harm after a few days and once the male has spun a further sperm web, to have another try. If the female was impregnated in the first mating she will refuse to have anything to do with the male a second time.

The description above is a 'copy-book' account of mating and, of course, it does not always work that way. Occasionally, a female will rush at the male, bite him and carry him off to her burrow. If she does this, there is nothing can be done—she will, I am afraid, eat him! This is a risk male tarantulas (and their owners) take to perpetuate the species.

From the many matings I have arranged/witnessed/ observed there are many deviations from the copy-book way. A pair of Giant Colombian Bird Eaters were mated in a large tank and the mating dance, drumming, was observed from both parties. The male then trundled over, lifted the female and hooked her fangs before she

Latrodectus pallidus, a species of Black Widow Spider (presumably dangerous to man) from the Near East.

Giant Colombian Bird Eaters mating.

had a chance to agree or otherwise. This pairing took a staggering 33 minutes, during which time he pushed her to every corner of the three-foot tank. The parting that I had been dreading with such aggressive spiders was gentle and almost friendly. The two simply broke apart and walked away from each other. From further experiences with these large spiders, it does appear they are less aggressive toward each other than they are toward their owners.

Mating a pair of Costa Rican Red Leg (*Brachypelma mesomelas*) is a torrid affair, if I may quote my friend Vince Hull-Williams, where aggression takes over before, during and after the pairing. Males need to be removed with due haste.

A pair of Costa Rican Zebra Tarantulas (*Aphonopelma seemanni*) can be the worst to get together. The males seem extremely reluctant despite having made all the normal male preparations. Get them together in a tank and you have problems, for nine times out of ten the female will be willing and the male quite the opposite. My own female of this species proved very keen and eager on one occasion and the same happened with the female of my friends Dennis and Carol, but the male—there was no way that any of us could persuade him to do his duty! From these observations, I can only conclude that Costa Rican Zebras are very hit-and-miss as far as reproduction is concerned.

The Haitian Brown (*Phormictopus cancerides*) is one of my favourite spiders but it appears that this particular species is unsure of its own gender. On two separate occasions a newly matured male was introduced to a female and on both occasions mating was perfect. However, a few days following the mating both the females moulted into mature males! The South American Pink Toe (*Avicularia avicularia*) caused us a few small problems when trying to get a male and female together. The male was tiny, as they often are, but nonetheless he was introduced into the female's container. After some two hours during which time the male drummed on the substrate, on her tube web, on the glass tank sides and virtually anywhere else he could think of, she finally decided to emerge. This she did and the male, unable to contain his impatience any longer, rushed at her, pushed her backwards, hooked her fangs and successfully completed the job. He then tried to get away but she had other ideas and

Above: A tailless whipscorpion with her young on her abdomen.

Opposite page: Lycosa poliostoma, a large South American wolf spider, with its egg ball.

we were prepared for a contretemps; however, he suddenly threw what I can only describe as a rabbit punch at her which had the effect of forcing her to twist and it was in this movement that the poor little male was literally tossed through the air, landing in an ungainly heap on his back at the bottom of the tank. She meantime had scuttled back into her web. We lifted the male out with no ill effects and he lived his life out quite happily.

The Mexican Red Knee (*Brachypelma smithi*) must be one of the easiest of all tarantulas to mate. I have mated something like ten pairs over the years and every single one has been copy-book. The problems occur, it appears, afterwards, since the females are supposed to be seasonal and can hold the sperm for up to a year, laying their egg sacs in the spring. On several occasions a female will moult after mating even though her cycle is perhaps months away. It can be very irritating.

The White Collared Tarantula (*Pterinopelma saltator*) is considered the most docile tarantula in the world today. It certainly seems friendly enough, and if it is taken from its tank to sit on a hand, it always seems reluctant to return to its tank. Therefore, I was completely unprepared for what transpired when I was offered the use of a male of this species. My adult female was beautiful and had recently moulted so, having followed the feeding well rules, I promptly popped the male into her tank and sat back to observe. The mating appeared to proceed normally, but since they are small spiders it was hard to be certain that the male had been able to do his work correctly. The next thing I knew was a flurry of activities with the male in what could only be described as considerable panic because the female had decided she was hungry and would very much like to eat him. I managed to separate them and lifted the male from the tank and back into his container as quickly as possible! What followed was strange; the female literally roamed the tank for several minutes seemingly searching for her missed meal. She climbed the sides, something she very seldom does, she dug in the substrate, she pulled at the sphagnum moss and upended her water pot.

The reader will therefore realise from these notes that sometimes matings can be simply a pleasure, but sometimes they can be painful—especially for

Indian Ornamental Black
and White Tarantula,
Poecilotheria regalis.

the male tarantula. Having said that, breeding MUST be attempted and MUST continue.

Once the mating has taken place, the female will continue to feed normally for some time, until eventually (some six to nine weeks later on average) she will spin a mat of silk on the substrate into which she will lay globules of yellowy looking eggs. She will then wrap them up until they form a largish cotton wool ball that is the egg sac. The eggs hatch in anything from four to 16 weeks, and during the incubation period the female will seldom, if ever, leave them. She will not normally feed at all during this time.

It can be quite worrisome since she is thinner once the eggs are laid and appears to get even more anorexic as time goes by. This is nothing to worry about.

Eventually the eggs will hatch, and at this time you must remove the female tarantula to a new home for, if you do not, she will undoubtedly begin to eat her offspring. A small hole will appear near to the top of the egg sac through which the spiderlings will emerge. If it appears that they are having problems getting out you can assist them by snipping the sac gently with nail scissors to make the hole larger.

Now the best thing

to do is to fill the tank half full with sphagnum moss, which will enable the spiderlings to go their separate ways. They will have had their first moult inside the egg sac and after a week to ten days they will have their first moult outside. It is after this one that they will start to feed. The best food for this size of spider is either drosophila (fruit flies), which can be obtained from insect dealers, or micro-crickets, which, again, are commercially available. As long as you keep plenty of food in the tank with them, the spiderlings should live happily together for a few weeks. You will inevitably lose some; this is nature's way of weeding out the runts in the litter, so do not be discouraged.

The care of these babies is covered in the chapter on rearing spiderlings so I will not repeat myself here. Without doubt you will find considerable pleasure in bringing up these babies and there really will be little pain!

We have talked about maturing males and what to do when one matures in your collection. Until recently, it has been practically impossible to tell whether your spider is a male until this maturing moult. However, my friend and colleague, John Hancock, has come up with a foolproof method of sexing tarantulas using their moult

Red Rump Tarantula.

skins, and the following section will give you some clues as to how this can be achieved.

SEXING SPIDERS

(SEX DETERMINATION OF IMMATURE THERAPHOSID SPIDERS, by Kathleen and John Hancock)

In Great Britain, the British Tarantula Society has outlined one of its aims as 'to encourage and participate in a long-term captive breeding programme which will both relieve the pressure on the indigenous habitats and create a supply of reasonably priced specimens for the amateur arachnologist.'

For this aim to be fulfilled, the amateur arachnologist must not only breed tarantulas but also rear the resulting spiderlings to adulthood! This may seem a daunting task, but really it could not be simpler.

The whole breeding programme, however, depends on fresh mature males being available. Unfortunately, male theraphosids live for only 20 or so months at most once matured, and it is important that fresh males are made available *every* year since they are really only viable for a few months following their maturity. The only really practical way of doing this is to

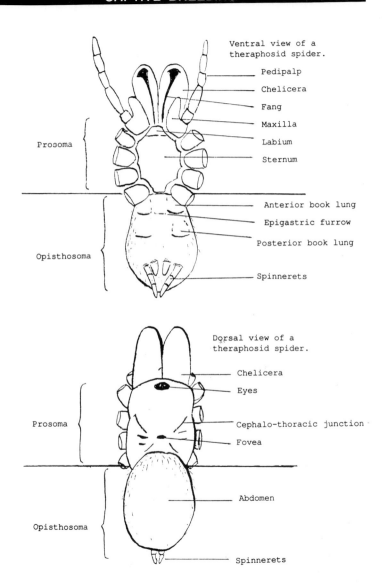

Ventral view of a
theraphosid spider.

Pedipalp

Chelicera

Fang

Maxilla

Labium

Sternum

Prosoma

Anterior book lung

Epigastric furrow

Posterior book lung

Opisthosoma

Spinnerets

Dorsal view of a
theraphosid spider.

Chelicera

Eyes

Cephalo-thoracic junction

Prosoma

Fovea

Abdomen

Opisthosoma

Spinnerets

rear spiderlings to adulthood.

Equally, it is important to know whether or not you have males at a very early stage, so the determination of the sex of a tarantula at an early age is essential and must be positive. In this way a great deal of wasted effort can be avoided. Young males can then be 'grown-on' at a rate that coincides with the coming into 'season' of the available females; thus the hit-or-miss methods of the past can also be avoided.

The body of a theraphosid, as in all spiders, can readily be seen to be divided into two parts. The anterior prosoma (or head region) carries the eyes, legs, etc. The posterior abdomen (or opisthosoma) carries the book lungs, spinnerets and the openings to the reproductive organs. The female's reproductive organs consist of a pair of ovaries and tubes that carry the eggs down to the exterior via an enlarged pocket (the uterus externus). From this pocket are two blind sacs in which the male's sperm is stored, known as the spermathecae. It will be appreciated at this point to consider the exoskeleton which is made up of a hard material called 'cuticle'. This hard and rigid exoskeleton of the spider rather limits the growth of its body.

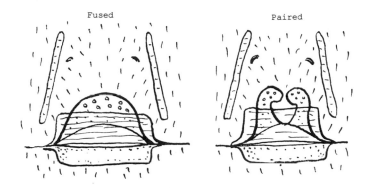

Fused   Paired

Two basic forms of spermatheca predominate in the Family Theraphosidae.

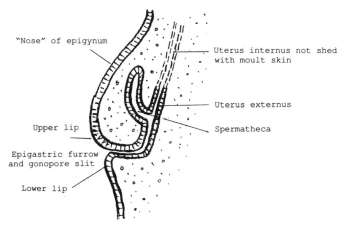

"Nose" of epigynum

Uterus internus not shed with moult skin

Uterus externus

Spermatheca

Upper lip

Epigastric furrow and gonopore slit

Lower lip

Side view of female's epigynum area

(a) Flip over onto back,
first tear begins
across clypeus

(b) Old skin continues
to tear laterally

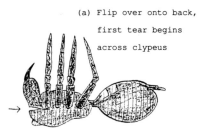

(c) Tear extends in abdomen

(d) Legs withdraw

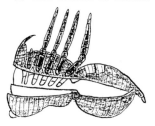

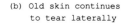

Process of theraphosid ecdysis

(e) Completed ecdysis; note lay-out of moult skin

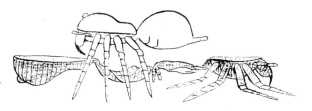

Thereby the actual growth can only occur directly after ecdysis (the shedding of the entire old skin—the moult). Everything on the outside is cast: all the hairs, spinnerets, claws, lens to the eyes and some parts of the insides too, including the book lungs, lining to the pharynx (throat) and the spermathecae. The new cuticle lies wrinkled beneath the old skin and can be stretched during and immediately after moulting. The spermathecae are lined with cuticle, as is the uterus externus pocket. In the theraphosids, which moult even in their adult stage, this lining is shed along with the old skin. This, in effect, means that any previously mated female becomes virginal again because any stored sperm will be lost with the moult skin.

It is also important to bear in mind that the presence of spermathecae establishes the fact that this particular spider is definitely female. Thus, the object in the determination of a spider's sex is to see if spermathecae are present or not in the old moult skin. The skin must be soft and flexible to enable its examination. The best method is to soak it in a solution of water and liquid soap, then gently untwist the abdomen skin.

Moult skin laid out for examination with the abdomen's ventral skin laid flat.

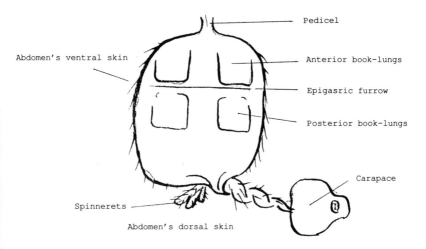

- Pedicel
- Abdomen's ventral skin
- Anterior book-lungs
- Epigasric furrow
- Posterior book-lungs
- Carapace
- Spinnerets
- Abdomen's dorsal skin

Abdomen's ventral skin laid out showing the epigynum area.

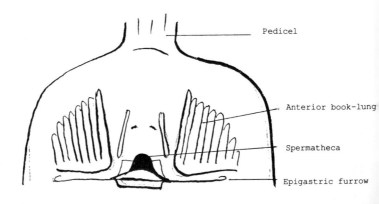

- Pedicel
- Anterior book-lung
- Spermatheca
- Epigastric furrow

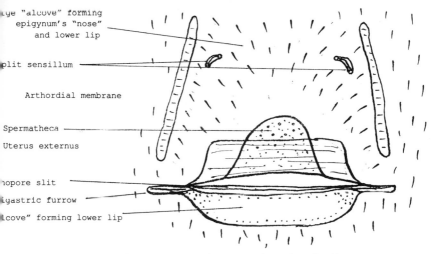

large "alcove" forming epigynum's "nose" and lower lip

split sensillum

Arthordial membrane

Spermatheca

Uterus externus

epigastric slit

epigastric furrow

"alcove" forming lower lip

Female epigynum area showing spermatheca from inside.

It is a good plan to lay the wet skin on a sheet of glass and try to arrange it so that the two pairs of book lungs can be seen. You will find that a lens of X10 will suffice for adult spiders, but to tackle the smaller spiderling a stereo microscope with a magnification range of X6 to X50 is required.

The next stage is to locate the anterior book lungs (the pairs nearest to the head). Between this pair will be found the epigastric furrow. Just above this crease, the part of the spider's sexual organs in which we are interested can be observed where the female's epigynum is displayed viewed from inside.

Male and female epigynum areas compared. (Viewed from the inside)

Female ♀

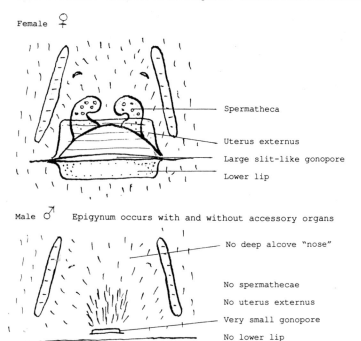

— Spermatheca

— Uterus externus

— Large slit-like gonopore

— Lower lip

Male ♂ Epigynum occurs with and without accessory organs

— No deep alcove "nose"

No spermathecae

No uterus externus

— Very small gonopore

No lower lip

Male epigynum with a pair of accessory organs.

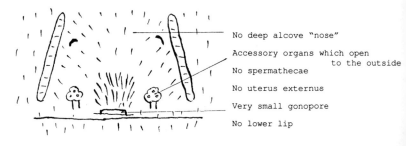

— No deep alcove "nose"

Accessory organs which open
to the outside

No spermathecae

No uterus externus

— Very small gonopore

No lower lip

Spermathecae come in two main types—paired or fused—but to understand just what you are looking for see the figure of a side view of the female's epigynum area.

In most species the female would be quite obvious, but to determine a male positively needs some experience owing to the presence, in some species, of accessory glands that can be easily mistaken for spermathecae. You can compare the spermathecae of the developing young female in her sixth moult with that of an adult male and its accessory gland.

Sex determination of spiderlings is a very important area that

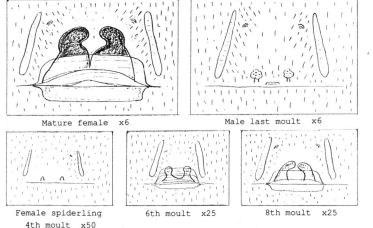

Mature female   x6

Male last moult   x6

Female spiderling
4th moult   x50

6th moult   x25

8th moult   x25

Aphonopelma seemanni.

offers great potential to the breeding of these wonderful spiders. Sex determination of moult skins as young as four months is possible; however, six months is a more practical age.

Once you have determined the sex of your spider, you can easily include him or her in a future breeding programme. Males of all species are eagerly sought after in captive breeding circles if you do not wish to attempt matings yourself.

If you find you do not have either time or inclination to study your spider's moults, then John Hancock will be pleased to help out. He runs a sexing service that costs a minimal amount and you can contact him at the address shown in the rear of this book, sending a stamped addressed envelope (in the United Kingdom) for his reply.

A close-up of a Striped Knee Tarantula.

Individual Species

The list printed earlier in this book gives the names of 38 species of tarantula that may be available in the pet trade; some are easy to obtain, some are not. With a few exceptions I have, or have had in the past, a specimen of each of the spiders listed and there follows a detailed guide giving colouration, natural habitat, etc., of these individuals. Wherever possible, a photograph or illustration has been included, thereby

Anatomy of a tarantula

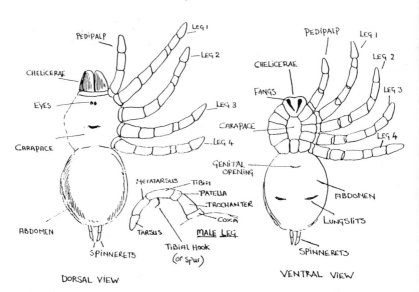

DORSAL VIEW

VENTRAL VIEW

giving a better idea of the species discussed.

Pamphobeteus sp.

BOLIVIAN STEELY-BLUE LEGGED BIRD EATER (*Pamphobeteus antinious*)

As its name suggests, this spider comes from Bolivia and is also found in Peru. Like most of the *Pamphobeteus* spiders it is a large aggressive individual with a voracious appetite. Although not the largest spider in the world, it is much sought after along with *P. insignis* and *P. fortis*.

There is much confusion concerning these three tarantulas; indeed, there is much confusion with all the large 'bird-eater' type spiders.

Pamphobeteus antinious is basically a large very dark brown spider with long hairs on the legs and abdomen. In natural light there is a distinctive blue sheen on the front two walking legs, pedipalps, chelicerae and carapace. Average leg span of an adult female is approximately 6".

This spider can in *no way* be handled—attempts have been made in the past by those of extreme courage (or stupidity!) but it really is foolhardy to try.

My own adult female, now demised, was typical of her species—large, aggressive and hungry! She died naturally of old age, which for these large spiders is around 12-15 years.

In the wild, *P. antinious* are found in the tropical rainforests where the humidity is high, around 80%. Like most captive-managed tarantulas, these survive well at temperatures between 70 and 75°F. Provided you follow the housing details given earlier and keep the spider humid, you will find this species easy to keep.

Although perfectly happy to feed upon large crickets, the occasional locust or pinkie mouse will not come amiss. An open water dish is essential.

Egg sacs usually hatch within 8-10 weeks of laying and the spiderlings are strange inasmuch as they resemble the British Wolf Spider (*Lycosa* sp.) but are jet black; spindly legs give the impression of walking being hard work, however they move incredibly fast. They are larger than the average spiderling and grow rapidly, surviving happily at temperatures around 75°F.

CAMPINA GRANDE SALMON PINK BIRD EATER (*Lasiodora parahybana*)

This is another 'biggie' and, in some respects, resembles the Honduras Curly Hair (*Brachypelma albopilosa*) in that it has long curly hairs on the legs and abdomen. Basically, again, these are dark brown spiders but they stand out from the crowd of large bird-eater types by the curly hairs that are profusely pink. Adults also have a distinctive pink tinge on the carapace that is more prominent in males, who resemble a fluffy pink hairbrush!

To look at and admire this spider is fabulous, but its temperament belies its beauty. These are *EVIL!* They will attack even drops of water when their tanks are being sprayed. Human fingers, therefore, have

This drawing shows a tarantula in a threat position.

no chance against this demonic fang-swinging individual. *L. parahybana* is particularly keen on escapology as a hobby and has the ability to lift even the heaviest of lids.

Coming from the Campina Grande area of Brazil, their natural habitat is the rainforests. Deep substrate is necessary and humidity around 80%. Feeding should consist of large prey, i.e., large crickets, locusts, cockroaches, etc., and an open water dish is essential. *L.*

parahybana survives well in captivity, needing a temperature around 70/75°F. The lifespan of adult females is again 12-15 years.

I have no data on spiderlings of the species, but whether adult or spiderling, remember—these are aggressive spiders and be very careful and

***Grammastola cala*, Chilean Beautiful Tarantula.**

alert when attending to their needs!

CHILEAN BEAUTIFUL TARANTULA
(*Grammostola cala*)

In many ways this spider appears to be closely related to the Chilean Common Tarantula. By their wild collection site data, it appears they are different. Once studied in detail, the colouration of each species is definitely at variance.

The Chilean Beautiful Tarantula is a basic creamy brown with pale pinkish hairs on legs and abdomen. The carapace is a definite pink. Considered docile in temperament, this spider was primarily introduced into the pet trade as one of the alternatives for the Mexican Red Knee when that species became difficult to obtain. However, from personal experience, I have discovered that *G. cala* can, when the mood takes it, be slightly aggressive although perhaps that is too strong a word. Care and caution need to be exercised since I have found these to be more unpredictable than any of the 'docile' species.

It is very easy, without expert eyes, to confuse the two species of the Chilean 'Rose'.

As its name clearly suggests, *G. cala* come from Chile and is widely distributed throughout its native land. However, it resides mostly in the coastal rainforests and experience has shown that these spiders do like to burrow. Again from experience, I have found that G. cala is inclined to be more docile if kept at slightly lower temperatures than those often recommended. A high of 70/75°F seems to suit them best. Humidity needs to be around 70-80% and they feed, moult and live quite happily.

I cannot really recommend handling for G. cala unless absolutely necessary. Certainly they are less skittish than their cousins and it is possible to lift them by hand provided you are careful and follow the guidelines on handling.

Egg sacs have been shown to hatch within 6-10 weeks of laying and the spiderlings are relatively small, mainly pink in colour with black abdomens. I have found them fairly hard to rear and they do need a slightly higher temperature, say 75-80°F. Lifespan is around 12 years, males maturing at 2 years of age.

Feeding consists of medium to large crickets, small locusts, moths. An open water dish is essential.

CHILEAN COMMON TARANTULA (*Grammostola spatulata*)

Like its cousin G. cala, this tarantula originates in Chile where it is distributed around Valparaiso.

Grammostola spatulata, Chilean Common Tarantula.

Unlike *G. cala* this spider digs only shallow burrows in a Mediterranean-type habitat where humidity is around 75%. In captivity it should be given a deep substrate into which it can burrow should the desire take it. An open water dish should be provided and a temperature around 70°F is ideal.

The Chilean Common Tarantula is basically a soft coffee-coloured spider with creamy-pink hairs. Its carapace is brown and the pink sheen described for *G. cala* is absent in this species.

Although *G. spatulata* is considered docile, I would not advocate handling unnecessarily. They have been noted as being skittish and inclined toward dashing away! From my experience, they tend to show aggression if suddenly disturbed, rearing up into a threat position before running in the opposite direction!

Life span for adult females is around 12 years and males mature around 2 years of age. Breeding these spiders has been quite successful and the spiderlings are far hardier than those of *G. cala*, giving a higher survival rate.

Egg sacs hatch around 6-10 weeks after laying and the spiderlings are pink with black abdomens. They are slightly larger (perhaps a millimeter!) than those of *G. cala*.

Feeding consists of medium to large crickets, small locusts, moths.

CHILEAN YELLOW RUMP (*Phryxotrichus auratus*)

Here we go with the third 'Chilean Rose' and the cause of much confusion. If you ignore the colour of the spider (not an easy task!) or see them without the close presence of either *G. cala* and/or *G. spatulata*, at first

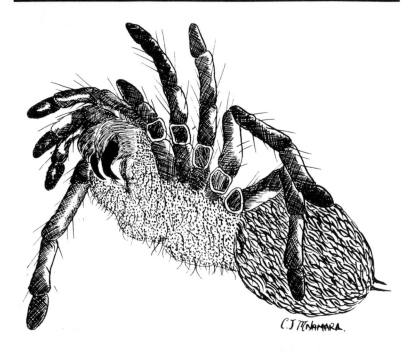

C.J M°NAMARA.

Phryxotrichus auratus, Chilean Yellow Rump.

glance you could be forgiven for thinking them to be a Common or a Beautiful Chilean. In fact, as seen by the scientific name, it is neither.

It is, of course, another Chilean spider and is found in areas around Santiago and Valdivia. It has also been found in Peru. From collection sites the natural habitat is the mountain scrubland where it appears contented with humidity at 75% and a temperature around

70°F. Again a fairly deep substrate should be provided and an open water dish. I have found this species not at all easy to keep and they seem to die for no special reason. Even when all the conditions are what would be considered perfect, the spider is found one morning as dead as dead can ever be. Several of my specimens that have ended up in this way have been passed over to the researchers and hopefully someone will come up with a reason for this untimely demise. In the meantime, one can only endeavour to imitate the natural habitat as closely and succinctly as possible.

Feeding these spiders will take medium to large insects, i.e., locusts, crickets, moths.

The 'Yellow Rump' name is slightly misleading since there does not appear to be any yellow present in the colouration. The tarantula is basically dark brown-red with a profusion of orange hairs covering the legs and abdomen. It has rather an ungainly gait and appears to spend most of its time standing 'tiptoe' in the centre of its tank. Why it does this is a complete mystery.

P. auratus does not appear to show any aggression when human hands are in the vicinity; each of my specimens has behaved identically when I have been attending to their needs, remaining on tiptoe, lying flat down to the substrate or strolling away into a corner. It does seem to have a pleasant enough temperament.

Spiderlings have been successfully reared and hatching occurs between 6-10 weeks from the date of the egg sac being laid. The spiderlings are identical to those of *G. cala* and *G. spatulata* (and quite a number of other species too!), being pink with black abdomens. They are fairly small at emergence but appear to grow quite rapidly. There are no data on female life spans but we can, I feel, assume that in normal circumstances this would be around 12 years with males probably maturing around 2-3 years of age.

COBALT BLUE (*Melopoeus/ Haplopelma lividus*)

This enigma can be considered evil tempered! Originating in Burma, it is a near relative of the Thailand Black (Edible) Tarantula. It lives in deep burrows that it lines completely with silk from every conceivable direction. The natural habitat is the rainforest areas and therefore a high humidity of around 85% is required in captivity, but a temperature of 70/75°F is adequate.

Haplopelma lividus, Cobalt Blue.

When first described to me as a 'blue' spider, my initial thoughts were 'Oh, sure, I've seen blue spiders before!' I was, thus, totally unprepared when the spider arrived. To my utter amazement, on opening the parcel I was confronted by a rearing fang-wielding individual clothed almost entirely in royal blue suit; the iridescent sheen on all eight legs and carapace shows in natural light to be striking (and I don't mean its fangs!)—so I had my 'blue' spider!

Like all Old World tarantulas, the Cobalt Blue has an elongated body with a slimmish abdomen that is chocolate brown in colour. The carapace is light fawn going on tan around the eyes. Again like other Old World tarantulas, it is very aggressive and will strike out at anything and everything that moves in the tank, including water!

Of all the tarantulas I have seen, from the colouration point of view, this is the most beautiful but it is certainly one of the nastiest. However, it is easy to keep feeding well on large crickets.

An open water dish is preferable.

I have no data on breeding this species although it has been attempted in the U.K. No results have yet been forthcoming.

If you want an unusual tarantula, this is it.

COLOMBIAN GIANT BIRD EATERS (*Xenethis/ Acanthoscurria/ Pamphobeteus* spp.)

Without wishing to enter the great debate as to just which species these large spiders are, they still have a place in this book. In fact, some people will buy a spider only if it is of gigantic proportions. Thus they are kept in captivity and need to be kept properly.

Coming from Colombia (*Xenethis*); Brazil, Argentina (*Acanthoscurria*); Colombia, Brazil, Ecuador, Bolivia (*Pamphobeteus*), these are *all* very large spiders.

Their natural habitat is the tropical rainforests, where they burrow into the undergrowth. A high humidity is required, around 80%, and a temperature of 75°F should be sufficient in captivity.

The spiders sold some two or so years ago, as spiderlings, were designated at the time *Xenethis monstruosa* and are now beginning to mature although my own specimen is still subadult. Some have been thought to be *Pamphobeteus fortis*, but there is still little data yet available to confirm the identification of this species.

Being large spiders, they need to eat large food and will take locusts and crickets with an occasional pinkie mouse.

Without exception they have been proved as aggressive and 'scared of no one' so that attempting to handle is not a good idea. It has been tried in the past and failed miserably.

These are really collectors' spiders and I would not recommend them as pets.

They need an open

water dish. Their lifespans appear to be 12-15 years.

COLOMBIAN PURPLE BLOOM BIRD EATER (*Pamphobeteus insignis*)

Of all the species in the 'Giant' categories this one has proved the most docile in my experience. My female adult never gave cause for alarm and belied all the reports of 'nasty' tempered with these huge spiders.

P. insignis is distributed around Cauca in Colombia, its natural habitat consisting of rainforests where exists a high humidity. Imitate this in captivity to around 80% and you cannot go wrong. It needs a deep substrate and an open water dish and will survive at 70-75°F.

In colour this basically is a light chocolate brown with an incredible purple sheen on the two front walking legs, pedipalps, chelicerae and carapace. The males are more striking in colour and resemble *P. fortis*, which is also inclined to the purple appearance. The females have huge abdomens making it very difficult to discern whether or not they are gravid after matings. *P. insignis* spins web prolifically upon the ground of her tank but does not incline toward webbing above ground level.

P. insignis needs large prey, i.e., locusts,

Pamphobeteus insignis, **Colombian Purple Bloom.**

large crickets, pinkie mice, and an open water dish is essential.

Lifespan appears to be around 12-15 years.

COMMON ORANGE RUMP (*Citharacanthus longipes*)

This little demon is a small species and fairly aggressive. It will rear up for no apparent reason, often remaining in this position for several hours with fangs bared and ready.

C. longipes is found in Mexico and Guatemala, also in Costa Rica. It has been found in many differing habitats and a humidity of 75% should suit adequately. It survives well in captivity at around 70/75°F and needs a slightly smaller tank than those described in the chapter on housing. Something around 8" x 6" is ample. A small open water dish is needed. The spider will feed upon medium to large crickets, small moths, etc.

The colour is pale brown-beige with a distinct orange underside. The classic stance for the spider is as described above. Handling? Don't try it!

Lifespan is probably around 10-12 years. I have no data on breeding in captivity.

COSTA RICAN BLUE FRONT (*Citharacanthus crinirufus*)

As far as is known, these spiders reside in tropical rainforests with a high humidity around 80%. In captivity a temperature between 70 and 75°F should suit.

This is a blue-grey spider with a chocolate brown abdomen and cream bands on the leg joints. The chelicerae have a very distinct blue 'patch'. This is again a smallish species and has been reported as aggressive. My female belies this as she has never shown any signs of being nasty-tempered.

Provide a deep substrate for *C. crinirufus* and she will

be happy digging and changing things around. A small open water dish and the normal food insects of medium to large crickets, moths, etc., are ideal.

Handling: Basically I don't advise it, for this is one of the unpredictable spiders and chances should not be taken.

COSTA RICAN RED LEG (*Brachypelma mesomelas*)

This is yet another species that has been brought into the U.K. as an attempt to woo tarantula keepers away from the Mexican Red Knee and, on the face of it, it seemed a good idea. However, this is a more aggressive species and although

Brachypelma mesomelas, Costa Rican Red Leg.

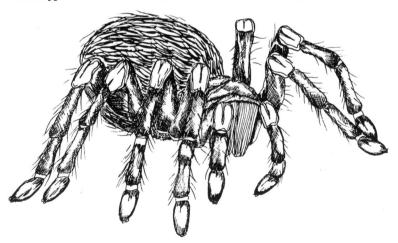

C.J.McNamara.

its markings are very similar and very attractive, expectations have not been realised.

I have found this spider hard to keep, i.e., early death seems a problem. Although imitating the natural habitat as closely as possible, I have yet to raise *B. mesomelas* beyond juvenile stages. Others have had success with this species, however.

B. mesomelas originates in the tropical rainforests of Costa Rica where it

Citharacanthus crinirufus, **Costa Rican Blue Front.**

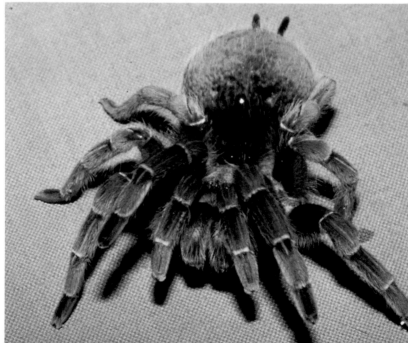

burrows deeply into the undergrowth. It needs a high humidity of around 80% and should survive happily at 75°F.

This is a dark brownish-black tarantula with red hairs that are especially thick on the legs, giving rise to its common name. It has been relatively easy to come by and is being bred in captivity.

Spiderlings are quite small and pink with black abdomens, looking nothing like their adult counterparts. They appear to be quite hardy up to juvenile stages, when all the problems of early death have occurred. From data available B. mesomelas should live to around 12 years of age.

B. mesomelas feeds erratically; in other words sometimes it will strike immediately and other times ignore or even flick away a potential dinner. An open water dish is essential as I wonder whether desiccation could be a cause of some of the deaths.

Metriopelma zebrata, Costa Rican Sun Tiger Abdomen.

COSTA RICAN SUN TIGER ABDOMEN (*Metriopelma zebrata*)

This again is quite a small tarantula but quite beautifully marked, being basically dark brownish-black with a flamingo-pink carapace making a startling contrast to its orange and black tiger-striped abdomen. Even spiderlings have their colours, but it has been noted that as the spiders go beyond maturity, the tiger stripes disappear.

Being small makes *M. zebrata* an aggressive mini-beast, and it moves like lightning when disturbed. It feeds well on medium crickets, small moths, etc., and a tiny open water dish is necessary.

M. zebrata is widely distributed in Costa Rica through the rainforests and high humidity is important—around 80/85%; again this spider does well in captivity around 75°F. Males of this species do not have the tibial spurs or mating hooks on the front pair of walking legs, although other male characteristics are identical to those of more typical tarantulas.

This is a spider well worth searching for and once installed in a small tank (8" x 6" maximum) it will dig and burrow and silk line as it goes. A really fascinating creature.

COSTA RICAN ZEBRA (*Aphonopelma seemanni*)

Yet another rainforest species distributed widely throughout its native land and sometimes found in Nicaragua, Honduras and southern parts of Mexico. The Costa Rican Zebra burrows deeply into the undergrowth in tropical environments and is, apparently, easy to persuade out of its burrow on collecting trips.

Another most attractive spider and one that it was originally thought would replace the Mexican Red Knee (*Brachypelma smithi*) in the pet trade. This didn't completely work out mainly because the Zebra Tarantula could be described as fairly skittish and not that easy to deal with.

It is nonetheless a beautiful spider, basically black with very distinctive cream 'zebra' stripes down all leg segments; the black tends to fade down to a lightish brown prior to moulting, but after this event the spider is striking in appearance.

It does make a delightful addition to any collection although its skittishness sometimes seems like aggression. They tend to run—rapidly—rather than attack when frightened. Because of this tendency, it is ill-advised to try handling for the very skittish behaviour puts the life of the spider in

Aphonopelma seemanni,
Costa Rican Zebra.

jeopardy. Females of the species have a life span around 12-18 years and males mature between 2 and 3 years of age. *A. seemanni* have proved a breeder's nightmare, but if you can get them to mate the egg sac once laid is usually guarded zealously by the female throughout the 8-10 weeks incubation period. Spiderlings when emerging are, like many others, pink with black legs. They feed well almost from the start, i.e., after their first moult outside the egg sac, and grow rapidly, obtaining their adult colours at about 6-10 months of age.

A. *seemanni* survive well at 70-75°F and humidity needs to be around 80%. They feed upon crickets, small locusts, moths, etc., and an open water dish is vital.

The Costa Rican Zebra is a classic tank-wrecker! It will dig out whatever is placed in its tank right down to the glass bottom. When setting up your tank for these tarantulas, don't bother with landscaping; it won't last long enough to warrant the time and effort put into it. Even tiny spiderlings do their housework!

EAST AFRICAN HORNED BABOON (*Ceratogyrus darlingi*)

If it can be obtained, this is a very nice addition to anyone's collection. It must be noted, however, that here we have a very aggressive and demonic spider. It lurks! You should also take into account that you probably won't see much of the spiders since, invariably, they disappear into the silk-lined and encrusted burrow that they dig for themselves. Once again landscaping is not worth doing!

C. darlingi is very attractive, basically

Ceratogyrus darlingi, East African. Horned Baboon.

light fawny-brown with a distinctive hump on the carapace giving rise to its name 'horned' baboon. Colour varies slightly depending on collection areas.

Originating in Zimbabwe, this spider has been found at Enkeldoorne and also in Mozambique, where its natural habitat is the tropical rainforests. Humidity therefore needs to be high, around 80%. This spider does well at 70-75°F.

Spiderlings appear hardy and grow fairly rapidly. Like their adult counterparts, they dig, burrow, and web profusely in and around the area.

As long as you remember that these tarantulas are aggressive, all will be well.

ENTRE RIOS TARANTULA (*Grammostola iheringi*)

This relatively small species is one I am particularly taken with. My spiderling grew rapidly and soon became an adult female. When I was offered a male of the species I was, of course, delighted. However, two attempts at mating proved fruitless; the female just did not want to know. I decided to have a final try and left them overnight in a divided tank. In the morning I was amazed to find the female moulting (completely out of her annual cycle). Imagine my chagrin, however, when she finally completed the moult and stood up on all eight legs a delightful though rather angry male! This goes to prove the importance of having one's spiders sexed at an early age, leaving nothing to chance!

However, these spiders are attractive and interesting, having a basic dark brown colour but the abdomen is covered in long, clearly visible, red hairs. From the patella (knee) down, the legs have pale cream lines.

G. iheringi originate around the Rio Grande, Taquare, Brazil areas and burrow in tropical mixed forests where the humidity is around 75%. I found this species survived well at 70-75°F.

The Entre Rios Tarantula feeds upon medium crickets, moths, small locusts and most of the normal insect food. A small open water dish is essential.

Grammastola iheringi, **Entre Rios Tarantula.**

There are no reliable data upon lifespans nor upon breeding this species.

GOLIATH BIRD EATER (*Theraphosa leblondi*)

Here we have what is considered the largest theraphosid in the world. It most certainly is a 'biggie' with an appetite and temperament to match! There is no point in offering *T. leblondi* anything smaller than an adult locust for dinner and often it will take several daily! If you keep *T. leblondi* it is advisable to breed locusts as well! A pinkie mouse occasionally is another good food source.

Because of its size, *T. leblondi* is much sought after although, as far as its colouration is concerned, it is basically a chestnut brown spider and very hairy.

It has the ability to hiss when disturbed, the sound clearly audible. It originates in Surinam, Guyana, Brazil, and Venezuela, where it burrows in swampy ground. In very wet seasons they can be spotted at night sitting upon hummocks waiting for the floods to subside; in the drier season they burrow to obtain humidity as much as security. It is not now considered necessary to imitate these swampy conditions to the letter in captivity. Indeed, I was one of

Therophosa leblondi, **Goliath Bird Eater.**

the main instigators of swampy conditions for these spiders. However, having now kept one I have found that as long as you keep the spider warm (around 75°F) and humid to around 80%, making sure a large open water dish is always available, they survive very well. The main problem with keeping *T. leblondi* over-humid is making certain you keep the temperature well up to match. Such a large spider, of course, needs a larger than usual tank and I keep mine in a tank 18" x 12" with a sliding glass lid for feeding and watering. The substrate I now use for *T. leblondi* is the same as for all my spiders, i.e., vermiculite that is around 3" deep. A large piece of cork bark in one corner covered with sphagnum moss and an outside water pot are the only other furnishings.

Certainly these spiders cannot be handled nor should handling be attempted. I would not recommend this species for a beginner tarantula keeper, but for the experienced collector it is considered almost a 'must'!

Lifespan is approximately 12 years and breeding this species has yet to be reported in captivity although I am aware it has been tried and if you have a male you must find a female. Males, incidentally, do not have tibial spurs on their front pair of walking legs.

HAITIAN BROWN (*Phormictopus cancerides*)

This is another aggressive spider originating in the West

C.J.M^cNAMARA.

Phormictopus cancerides, **Haitian Brown.**

Indies and having a wide distribution area from Haiti, Port au Prince, Lares, Anasa. Its natural habitat is tropical scrubland/rainforests where it burrows into the undergrowth. Humidity should be around 80% and a temperature of 70-75°F suits this species well.

The spider is a largish dark brown creature with an

attractive pink pubescence on the carapace. Its stance and generally its appearance give those who do not know the impression that *all* tarantulas are evil! It lurks, and has been known to attack water globules falling into the tank. Often, because of reasonable prices, these spiders are purchased by novices or those wishing to 'show off'. Quite often it has been recommended for a beginner and, up to a point, it could be debated that this recommendation is valid—but for one reason only: IT IS TOUGH! It is adaptable to many environs but needs the high humidity factor, and therefore is less likely to come to an untimely end at the hands of someone who does not really know what they are doing.

P. cancerides is very, very aggressive and certainly cannot be handled even by experts without the use of large, long forceps or a tub and piece of card.

It will eat virtually anything that moves like an insect but needs an open water dish for drinking. The Haitian Brown is a gorgeous spider to behold and is highly recommended as a show piece in anyone's collection.

Breeding is easy with this species and the spiderlings hatch without too much trouble some 6-12 weeks after egg sac production. Spiderlings

Poecilotheria regalis, Indian Ornamental Black and White.

grow rapidly and males mature around two years of age. Lifespans appear to be 12-15 years for adult females.

HONDURAS CURLY HAIR (*Brachypelma albopilosa*)

This is my favourite of all the tarantulas for several reasons. I like their enthusiasm for life, their enjoyment of their food, their friendly and non-aggressive nature and their extreme beauty.

Basically a dark brown spider, the Honduras Curly Hair has a profusion of pinkish-orange hairs covering the abdomen and legs and looking for all the world as if they have been blow-waved!

B. albopilosa originates in Honduras and Costa Rica, distributed widely throughout the latter and less widely in the former. Its natural habitat is the rainforests where the humidity is 80% and this must be imitated in captivity. It helps to add a clump of sphagnum moss or snake grass to the substrate when setting up home for the Curly Hair.

They have prolific appetites and will feed on most medium to large insects including crickets and locusts. An open water dish is essential.

They are easy to breed and make good mothers while the spiderlings are still

C.J.MᶜNAMARA.

Brachypelma albopilosa, **Honduras Curly Hair.**

within the confines of the egg sac. Once hatched, the mother will most certainly begin to eat the babies so she is best removed to a new tank. The baby spiders can then be left together for several weeks provided plenty of food is given and they have hiding places. *B. albopilosa* grow rapidly and males mature around two years of age. The average lifespan of females is around 12 years.

Poecilotheria regalis, **Indian Ornamental Black and White.**

If you absolutely *must* handle the *B. albopilosa*, it can be easy or extremely difficult depending upon the mood of the spider. Some individuals will walk willingly onto a hand and others will not. They do have the ability to jump and this must be taken into consideration for a fall would undoubtedly result in death. Basically, therefore, I am against handling this species.

It is, however, a pure delight and a spider I never want to be without in my collection.

INDIAN ORNAMENTAL BLACK AND WHITE (*Poecilotheria regalis*)

This is fabulous! Its colours are virtually indescribable but I *will* try! Basically a black and white spider with a pattern covering the abdomen, legs and carapace with yellow tinges on the legs and underside. It is incredible and really has to be seen to be believed.

Until recently, little was known about the Indian spiders and certainly few people actually had such a spider in their collections. Along with its cousins (i) Sri Lankan Ornamental Black and White (*P. fasciata*) and (ii) Ornamental Gooty Plain Leg (*P. metallica*), it has now been imported in small numbers into the U.K. Hopefully all three species will be bred successfully in captivity for every tarantula fancier should have at least one of the three species in their collection. I am fortunate in that I have both *P. regalis* and *P. metallica.*

P. regalis originates in southwestern India through the Nilgiri Hills and is also found in Sri Lanka. It lives in trees in the monsoon forests where it builds a web nest and can be all but invisible to the naked eye, making them difficult to locate in the wild.

It is considered aggressive, as indeed are *P. fasciata* and *P. metallica*, and the Indian and Sri Lankan natives are very scared of them. One must exercise care and caution therefore when dealing with these spiders. They move like greased lightning but once settled in a tall tank with a largish piece of cork bark or bogwood to make their nest against, they will be happy enough.

Feeding is easy as these spiders will take large locusts, crickets, moths, etc. Spiderlings will feed on flies, medium moths, medium crickets and small locusts. Spiderlings grow incredibly fast and although there are no data as yet available on lifespans, it is generally felt that *P. regalis* and her kin will live around 12 to 15 years. I do not give my tree spiders water dishes as such but spray their bark and/ or webs daily to enable them to obtain moisture as they would be able to in the wild.

MERGUI REDDISH BROWN (*Ornithoctonus andersonni*)

This large Old World tarantula originates in the rainforests of Burma, around Mergui, and has been much sought after since its arrival in the U.K. a few years ago. It is a large and aggressive spider, a prolific webber, building huge constructions almost filling the entire tank.

It has a voracious appetite and will take large prey, i.e., adult locusts, etc. An open water dish is essential. In captivity the temperature needs to be between 70-75°F but humidity is important at around 80%.

O. andersonni is also a bit of an enigma since it is thought, in some quarters, that it is not *O. andersonni* at all but *Chilobrachys andersonni* (the Kawkareet Mustard Tarantula), which originates from the same area and is also found in Bangladesh. Whichever species it is proved to be, it is still an attractive addition to a collection if only for the engineering miracles it performs using its spinnerets as the only tool.

Judging from our own specimen, it appears that this spider has some kind of reasoning power since she left a hole in the web sufficient for me to top up and change her water dish when necessary.

O. andersonni has, to my knowledge, not been bred in captivity as yet so I have no data on spiderlings and the rearing thereof. Its lifespan is probably around 12 years for adult females. It is certainly not to be handled.

Ornithoctonus andersonni,
Mergui Reddish Brown.

MEXICAN BLACK VELVET/RED RUMP (*Brachypelma vagans*)

This is one of my favourite spiders, living up to its common name with its beautiful black velvet appearance, the abdomen covered with a profusion of red hairs and the carapace with a ring of cream on the outer limits. It is truly gorgeous and has a reasonably docile temperament.

B. vagans originates in Mexico, where it has a wide distribution area throughout both

Mexico and Guatemala. This species, in the wild, is a deep burrower and will survive in captivity at around 70-75°F with a humidity of 75%. Although it burrows deeply in its natural habitat, these spiders do not necessarily do so in captivity. Deep substrate will give

Brachypelma vagans, **Mexican Black Velvet/Red Rump.**

them the opportunity to dig if they so desire.

Feeding: *B. vagans* takes large crickets, moths and small locusts with ease and an open water dish is important.

The Black Velvet can move quite quickly when it wants to, but does not appear especially aggressive. Breeding is easy and the female makes a good mother on the whole until the egg sac hatches.

Females can live approximately 15 years with males maturing around two years of age. Spiderlings grow rapidly for the first year and then appear to slow down. They obtain their adult colours around six months.

All in all, this is a delightful spider to own.

MEXICAN BLONDE/ PALOMINO (*Aphonopelma chalcodes*)

Often referred to as the Palomino Tarantula, here we have a Marilyn Monroe look-alike!! A true blonde and very attractive. The species on the whole appears timid to the extreme and runs at the slightest vibration. The spider is basically a light brown with shining golden tan reflections on the carapace and on the legs giving it this blonde appearance.

The species is wide-ranging throughout Arizona, Texas and

Mexico, where it resides in scrubland under a low humidity. A burrowing species, it should survive well at 70-72°F in captivity. I use the world 'should' advisedly since premature deaths in captivity of *A. chalcodes* appear fairly common, both in adult and subadult specimens. Changing the temperature either way, up or down, does not appear to do any good, and the only thing I can think of is that the deaths are due to parasites or to a too high humidity factor in captivity. To my knowledge *A. chalcodes* has not yet been successfully bred in captivity, so it is likely that all specimens available through the pet trade would have been wild-collected. Once males mature from these wild-collected stocks and breeding commences, more data will become available through the rearing of the resulting spiderlings.

When healthy and fit, *A. chalcodes* feeds well on large crickets, medium locusts, etc., and is an attractive addition to any collection. Handling is ill-advised since their skittish nature could well result in accidents.

MEXICAN RED KNEE (*Brachypelma smithi*)

What can one say about this species that has not been said before? The spider

Above: Aphonopelma chalcodes, **Mexican Blonde/ Palomino.**

Below: Brachypelma smithi, **Mexican Red Knee.**

epitomises everyone's idea of a tarantula— large, hairy and colourfully striped on the legs in shades of orange, tan and cream around the entire circumference. The basic colour is black/ dark brown with a profusion of orangey- red hairs on the abdomen. Gorgeous!

B. smithi is widely distributed throughout its native land

Top: **Brachypelma sp.**, the Flame Knee. *Bottom:* **Bruchypelma vagans**, the Mexican Black Velvet/Red Rump.

although it is becoming rarer and is placed on CITES II as a protected species. In theory, this means it should not be sold unless proof of captive breeding can be produced. Of necessity, breeding in captivity is now taking place on a grand scale and with some success, so that it is hoped the wild stocks will be preserved from the unscrupulous who still continue to plunder.

While breeding these spiders in captivity is considered vital for their preservation, it has to be said that these are not the easiest of spiders to produce egg sacs. They are extremely easy to mate and seldom have males come to grief at the hands of an aggressive female, but from collected data they do appear seasonal in their reproduction, i.e., the females only lay their egg sacs in the spring. If, for example, one mates a pair of *B. smithi* in the late summer/autumn/winter it is unlikely that the female will produce an egg sac until somewhere around March/April of the following year. The females have the ability to store the sperm for some considerable time, and if the female should moult between mating and egg sac production then she will not produce the eggs. Once an egg sac has been laid, female Mexican

Red Knees appear to be good and protective mothers. The spiderlings develop within the egg sac anything from 10-16 weeks and when they hatch are exceedingly tiny. These are the longest lived of the tarantulas (some females have been known to live 30 years) and therefore it follows that the spiderlings grow rather slowly. An adult male or female normally matures around 5 years of age.

Handling *B. smithi* has, for a number of years, been considered easy—even natural—but be warned, some individuals do not take kindly to this practice and are quite capable of showing aggression. Usually this aggression takes the form of scuffing out the hairs from the abdomen, which can cause rashes and, should they connect with the eyes, a nasty infection. This is the spider's first form of defence; its next move is to turn, rear up and strike! *Always* exercise care. My 'pet' tarantula (Cleo) is the exception that proves the rule, and even she is quite capable of having an 'off-day' and refusing to be handled. Fortunately she has never been awkward at important times—yet!

Most Mexican Red Knees will take large crickets, medium locusts, etc. Some will take a large fat-bodied moth as an alternative. Some will

Brachypelma emilia, **Mexican True Red Leg.**

where the humidity is low. In captivity a temperature of 70°F and 65% humidity should be adequate. Simply because it comes from a desert environment does not make it necessary to keep the spider on sand. This is a burrowing spider requiring facilities for so doing, and vermiculite plus sphagnum moss is ideal.

The mahogany brown abdomen has a profusion of red hairs, the legs being dark with red hairs on the tibia and patella of each leg. The carapace carries a distinctive triangular pattern that is dark brown and creamy peach toward the abdomen, giving it

not take locusts at all. They tend to be fussy eaters, often going without for long periods. An open water dish is best.

MEXICAN TRUE RED LEG (*Brachypelma emilia*)

This tarantula comes from semi-desert scrubland from Mexico to Panama, where it has a fairly wide distribution area and a peculiar 'painted' appearance.

From personal experience I have found that this spider is the exception to the annual moult rule for adults. I have two specimens, neither of which have shed their skins for two years. Several friends and colleagues have reported the same phenomenon.

Mating *B. emilia* is relatively easy but I have noticed that females show a great deal of aggression toward the male after mating; on one occasion I had to save the poor male from potential death. For my pains the male then proceeded to attack his

Pterinochilus murinus, **Mombasa Golden Starburst Baboon.**

rescuer, but both he and I survived the encounter with no ill-effects. Spiderlings are quire large, twice the size of those of *B. smithi*, and appear to be very hardy.

B. emilia will take large crickets, medium locusts and the occasional moth. An open water dish is vital.

Re: handling *B. emilia*—basically—don't! These are quite nasty tempered spiders and remember, they can *AND DO* bite from time to time!

MOMBASA GOLDEN STARBURST BABOON (*Pterinochilus murinus*)

This is one of the 'new' species available from captive breeding programmes through the U.K. It is certainly beautiful—of that there is no doubt. Its abdomen is patterned in spots and stripes on a yellowish background, the carapace is covered with golden hairs and is very attractive. This attraction, however, does not continue to its temperament, which is nasty! It is aggressive and demonic, always ready to rear up and threaten at the least provocation.

This Old World tarantula ranges throughout Kenya and also Equatorial Africa, where its natural habitat is mixed woodland with humidity 70-80%. It survives in captivity at

70-75°F. Although described as ground-dwelling, from my experience the spider obviously does not read the same literature as we do! My specimen has built a cocoon-like web in the topmost corner of its container in which it lives, moults, etc.

It is a very hungry species taking quite large prey without thinking. A small open water dish is necessary and the spider will climb down from its web to drink and to feed.

Breeding these spiders has proved extremely easy and the spiderlings are quite large, aggressive and fast growing.

PAMPAS TAWNY RED (*Grammostola pulchripes*)

This delightful little spider is another with which I have only recently become acquainted. A basically chocolate brown/black spider, it has a profusion of tawny red/pink hairs and distinct yellow lines down the legs.

G. pulchripes originates in Brazil, Panama and Peru where its natural habitat is the pampas and savannah areas where there is a temperature around 75°F and humidity around 75%. In captivity it burrows into vermiculite and appears to like sphagnum moss in which it can hide.

It is a fairly small tarantula and therefore medium crickets are ideal as food. A small open water dish is important.

G. pulchripes appears quite friendly and docile. I have no data on breeding although this is being attempted.

Grammostola pulchripes, **Pampas Tawny Red.**

SINGAPORE REDDISH BROWN (*Coremiocnemis validus*)

This is a spider with which I have little personal experience; however they are kept successfully in captivity and it appears they need even less space than other tarantulas.

In the wild it is found around Penang, Malaysia and Singapore and very occasionally in India. Its natural habitat is rainforest with a high humidity requirement around 80%. Temperature, in captivity, needs to be between 72-75°F and a substrate of vermiculite with sphagnum moss added is an asset.

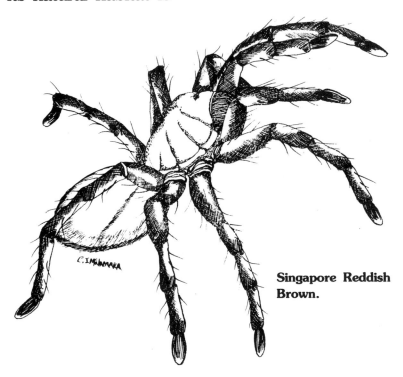

Singapore Reddish Brown.

The spider is blackish in colour with a yellow sheen and the abdomen is yellowish-brown, the legs are yellow brown. It will feed on the normal feed insects, i.e., crickets, medium locusts, etc. An open water dish is essential.

Its temperament has been described as aggressive and it is exceedingly skittish and fast moving.

SOUTH AMERICAN HORNED BABOON (*Spaerobothria hoffmanni*)

Here again I have little personal experience of this spider, but I gather they are easy to keep and very attractive.

Originating in Costa Rica, the spider is widely distributed around the Monteverde Reserve where its natural habitat is the rainforests where there is a humidity factor of 80%. Temperature needs to be around 70-75°F in captivity and a deep substrate will give the spider the burrowing facilities. Sphagnum moss helps with humidity.

Again a yellow-brown spider with a grey-brown sheen, the abdomen is dull brown-black and it has a very definite hump on the carapace.

Feeding: large crickets, medium locusts, etc.; an open water dish is essential.

Basically *don't* try to handle *S. hoffmanni*. I am told they are very,

very aggressive spiders and fast moving. Best play it safe.

SOUTH AMERICAN PINK TOE (*Avicularia avicularia*)

This arboreal (or tree) spider originates in the banana and/or pineapple plantations of Guyana, Trinidad and Brazil. It is abundant in Maroval, Trinidad and the valley of the Amazon River.

It is vital for their welfare in captivity that these spiders have tall containers with twigs or bark to which they can anchor their web nest. The nests are built in a tubular shape and are so thick as to be impossible to tear with the fingers, requiring very sharp scissors should it need to be cut open (e.g., to allow spiderlings out).

For *A. avicularia* it is unnecessary to provide water dishes but you must spray the webs every day to ensure (1) that they can drink naturally and (2) that the humidity is kept constantly high around 80/90%. These beautiful spiders are very prone to desiccation, which is the prime cause of death in nine out of ten of this species. They do well at a temperature of 70-75°F.

They prefer flying insects as prey but they will take large crickets, medium to large locusts. Moths appear to be a favourite food.

They are very easy to breed and the egg sac is laid inside the web nest, the mother guarding it zealously throughout the incubation period. Spiderlings are a negative of the adult, being pink with black shoes. Adults are jet black, like furry velvet, with pink toes that are almost red in males. Males are usually much smaller than females, which does not appear to cause them any problems in mating.

Above: **The long hairs on this Red Rump Tarantula possibly indicate that it is related to** *Avicularia* **sp.** *Opposite page:* *Avicularia avicularia,* **South American Pink Toe.**

These are docile, sweet natured creatures but have the ability to jump (12" from a standing position has been recorded!). However, once they have jumped they tend to remain still. The Pink Toe is an absolute delight and one that I would never want to be without.

SOUTH AMERICAN YELLOW BANDED (*Avicularia* sp.)

Little is known of the actual location sites of this spider although they are known to come from both Brazil and Peru. It is thought that, in fact, there are two species of Yellow Banded, one being *Avicularia variegata* and the other

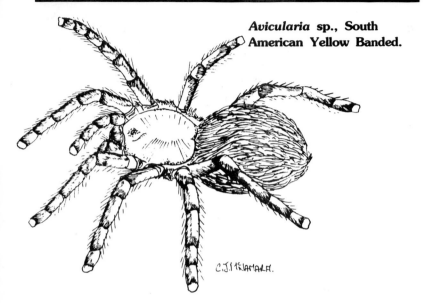

Avicularia sp., South American Yellow Banded.

C.J.MCNAMARA.

Avicularia magdalena. Clearly, they are definitely *Avicularia* species and their similarity to The South American Pink Toe is quite striking, despite their colour.

Again these are arboreal spiders needing a tall container with twigs or bark to which they can anchor their web nests. They seem to prefer prey that will either fly into their web (i.e., large moths) or climb up to the web (i.e., medium locusts) and for water it is important to spray their web daily which serves as drinking water and humidity aids. Temperature needs to be around 72-75°F and humidity around 80/90%.

This is a light to deep brown fluffy, furry spider with pinkish orange tips to the feet and very distinctive yellow bands around leg segments.

They appear slightly less docile than the South American Pink Toe and tend to strike out even at water globules dropping onto their webs. I do not, therefore, recommend attempting to handle this species.

TEXAS BIG BEND GOLD CARAPACE (*Eurypelma caniceps*)

Thought to be the Texas version of the Gold Orange Rump from Mexico, this species is prolific around the Big Bend area of Texas where its natural habitat is the scrubland area. Humidity needs to be around 75% and a temperature of 72/75°F appears ideal with this species.

Basically the spider is brownish-black, but its crowning glory is its very definite gold carapace that has a metallic sheen.

It is a hungry spider and leaps upon anything and everything that passes by. I have found them to be fairly aggressive and I would not suggest handling or even attempting to do so.

An open water dish is best.

As far as breeding is concerned, there has

Eurypelma caniceps, **Texas Big Bend Gold Carapace.**

been little done in this field to date. Spiderlings arrived in the U.K. in 1986 and males are beginning to mature, but the problem seems to be the procuring of females. *E. caniceps* is a slow grower and a slow and deliberate mover.

TEXAS BROWN (*Dugesiella hentzi*)

This is a common species in Texas and Arizona and is also found in Oklahoma, where males can be observed in the breeding season trudging along the highways. Their natural habitat is the scrubland desert where humidity is around 70% and the temperature around 72°F. Again a burrowing spider, this is also the one most likely to suffer from the parasitic wasp (the Tarantula Hawk).

A very deep brown spider with tan-red carapace and dark

brown-black legs, this is a spider with uncertain temperament but has been stated as aggressive. Handling therefore is not advised!

It will feed on medium to large crickets, medium locusts, etc., and an open water dish is best.

Above: Dugesiella hentzi, **Texas Brown.**

Right: Haplopelma minax, **Thailand Black.**

THAILAND BLACK (*Melopoeus/Haplopelma minax*)

Since I wrote "Wall to Wall Spiders" and described this spider in the Field Guide as *Melopoeus albostriatus*, further research has shown that this particular group of Old World tarantulas belong not to *Melopoeus* but to *Haplopelma*. Additionally, 'albostriatus' clearly means 'Striped' and therefore *H. albostriatus* is the Thailand Zebra and not the Thailand Black. This latter is now placed as *Haplopelma minax*—the Edible Tarantula!

The spider originates in the bamboo forests of Thailand and Burma and is an aggressive beast. A black spider with olive-black abdomen and slightly white tips to the feet, it often has slight chevron patterns on the abdomen. It is extremely attractive with the classic Old World elongated appearance.

This species is not recommended for beginners because of its ability to escape, its aggressive nature and its need for high humidity. Definitely *NOT* to be handled. Spiderlings, from my experience, are just as aggressive and nasty in temperament as the adults!

An open water dish is essential for this species and also the Thailand Zebra, whose

Melopoeus/Haplopelma albostriatus, the Thailand Zebra.

conditions and natural habitat are the same as the Thailand Black.

TIGER RUMP DOPPELGANGER (*Cyclosternum fasciata*)

This spider is now being successfully captive bred. Although at one time confused with *M. zebrata* (Costa Rican Sun Tiger Abdomen), it has now been classified correctly confirming that there are two species with bumble-bee abdomens. The main difference is that *C. fasciata* males have tibial spurs while *M. zebrata* males do not!

These are very small tarantulas but absolutely delightful and the spiderlings are also sweet but almost micro-cricket size! They grow rapidly and take on their adult colours very early in life, the tiger striped abdomen being very prominent.

A Costa Rican species, the habitat is the rainforests. A humidity of 80% is important, and a temperature around 72-75°F should suffice. These are burrowing spiders and usually make silk cocoon-like burrows in the substrate. They feed on small to medium crickets and require a small open water dish.

TRINIDAD CHEVRON (*Psalmopoeus cambridgei*)

This spider originates in Trinidad, in the West Indies and

Cyclosternum fasciata, **Tiger Rump Doppelganger.**

is widely distributed throughout. Its natural habitat is the silken tubes that it builds in folded leaves and even around buildings. A tall container is required for *P. cambridgei* and twigs or bark to which it can anchor its web nest. Humidity should be kept fairly high around 80% and you can achieve this and provide drinking water by spraying the nest daily. Temperature needs to be 70-75°F.

The Trinidad Chevron, like other arboreal spiders, seems to prefer to take food on the wing, i.e., large moths, but it will certainly take crickets and locusts as an alternative for it has a voracious appetite.

This is basically a light brown spider with fairly fluffy legs and very distinct chevron markings on the abdomen. In natural light, it has a gorgeous green sheen on legs and underside of the abdomen. It is long-legged and very fast moving. It tends toward aggression, therefore *don't* try to handle!

Mating is easiest of all since the male, when introduced into the female's tank, will sit and wait for her to emerge from her cocoon. When she does so, mating is rapid and

A close-up view of the patellas of a Mexican Red Leg Tarantula, *Brachypelma smithi.*

she will retreat almost immediately back to her cocoon. The incubation time for the egg sac is around six to eight weeks and the spiderlings are quite large, black with creamy pink socks. They are extremely hardy and very fast growing, reaching subadult size in only a few months.

Although aggressive, this spider is a superb addition to any collection.

TRINIDAD MAHOGANY BROWN (*Tapenauchenius plumipes*)

This species originates in Trinidad but sites have also been located in Surinam. The natural habitat is tropical

plantations where the spiders spin their web nests in the folds of leaves. Obviously, this is another arboreal

A Trinidad Mahogany Brown Tarantula, *Tapenauchenius plumipes*, stalks its food.

spider and therefore needs a tall container with twigs or bark to which can be anchored the web nest. A fairly high humidity of around 80% and a temperature of 70-75°F are needed. The humidity can be kept to the correct level by spraying the web nest daily, which will also give the spider facilities for drinking. Again, I have found these spiders prefer to take food on the wing, i.e., large moths, but they certainly will come out of their webs to chase both large crickets and medium locusts.

The spider is basically brown with a reddish abdomen, the male much smaller than the female. Inclined to be fast moving, this spider is a great escapologist and fairly aggressive by nature.

Handling this species is certainly *not* advisable. Friends had a large adult female who managed to escape while I was visiting. It was a source of great amusement when I, the experienced spider keeper, jumped back rapidly! Care, therefore, should be exercised when dealing with *T. plumipes*.

TRINIDAD OLIVE BROWN SPIDER (*Hapalopus incei*)

This is a tiny tarantula with whom I have only recently become acquainted. As their name suggests, they come from

Hapalopus incei, **Trinidad Olive Brown Spider.**

Trinidad, where they are very common indeed. It is found in tropical scrublands where it burrows, webbing as it goes and leaving holes in its web where it lurks waiting for prey. For something so small it is incredibly pretty. It is almost entirely brown in colour with olive hairs on the legs and abdomen. It has bands of brownish-black around the abdomen and the carapace has a golden sheen with what I can only describe as a starburst design.

These spiders need only a very small container but with a deep substrate so that the web can be constructed.

Again because of their small stature, they need only medium crickets but a tiny open water dish is important.

I mated a pair of these super spiders last year and found that to induce the male to approach the female required the upping of the temperature. This was achieved by placing the tank containing both spiders on my snake tank, where the heat coming up through the substrate achieved the desired result. The egg sac was duly laid and hatched within 3 weeks, which is unusual for tarantulas. The spiderlings appeared to be rather large for such a small adult and such a tiny egg sac. As they have developed the reason for this has become apparent; they grow rapidly and mature around 15 months!

As far as temperament is concerned, they are fairly aggressive little beasts and as they are so small it is

Pterinopelma saltator, **the White Collared Tarantula. The male is on the right, female on the left.**

impossible to handle them anyway.

WHITE COLLARED (*Pterinopelma saltator*)

Here we have what I consider the most docile of tarantulas, certainly the most docile of those with whom I have had contact. They seem incapable of showing aggression toward their owners and appear to love to walk on hands in their tanks, being reluctant to go back onto substrate.

They originate in Uruguay and Argentina where they are fairly widely distributed although they are now under a certain amount of protection and are no longer imported. Their natural habitat is the pampas plains where they burrow down in humidity of 75% and a temperature around 75°F. A deepish substrate enables them to burrow down at will.

The White Collared Tarantula is a strange two-tone spider, a light to mid-brown abdomen and rear legs, the front legs and carapace being light grey-fawn with a distinct 'collar' of cream around the carapace and leg joints. They do not grow very large but are utterly delightful in any collection.

Mating is easy, being simply a matter of putting them together and parting them gently afterward. They show very little aggression toward each other. Even their food appears to receive an apology before the spider leaps upon it. I provide my White Collared with an open water dish and a nice heap of sphagnum moss in which she can burrow if she so desires.

An unidentified tarantula, possibly an *Aphonopelma*, from Mexico.

Although the bite of most tarantulas is nearly harmless, there are some species that are truly venomous and dangerous to man. Tarantulas of the genus *Atrax*, a different family from the common hobby tarantulas, are common in Australia and have on occasion caused human deaths. An antivenin is available.

Odd Topics

REGENERATION

Many creatures in the zoological world have the remarkable ability to regenerate limbs and other parts of the body, i.e., tails in some geckos and rodents and the now famous story of the worm that grows another half on each severed segment thus becoming two, if sliced by the garden spade.

Spiders are adept at regrowing their limbs. If a leg, or part thereof, is lost through a fall or a fight, the limb will be regenerated in the next moult. The regenerated limb is not immediately very strong, having a thin appearance, and is fairly colourless, but this will improve moult by moult until no difference can be noticed from any of the other seven legs.

The pride and joy of my collection at present is an adult South American Pink Toe (*Avicularia avicularia*). When she came to me, she was minus two legs and one pedipalp and to be honest I did not hold out much hope for her. At the time she was a juvenile. She walked crab-like and somehow managed to snare her prey with her one remaining pedipalp, but she always looked clumsy and uncomfortable. Finally, she ceased to feed and

Citharischius crawshayi,
Kinani Rusty-Red Baboon.

went to the bottom of her container (unusual for a tree spider to be on the ground) where she remained for almost two weeks without moving at all. I was very concerned for her but there was nothing I could do except to let nature take its course and keep her nice and humid. Imagine, therefore, my utter delight one morning when I found she had moulted successfully and had regenerated all her missing appendages; a huge achievement. She has just quite simply got stronger and stronger until now she is a perfect specimen of her species!

Spiders are truly remarkable.

ALL CREATURES GREAT AND SMALL

Large spiders, small spiders—there are many differing and very interesting species. A large female *Lasiodora*

Avicularia avicularia, **South American Pink Toe.**

klugi collected in Brazil in 1945 weighed-in at three ounces, and now an even larger spider has achieved recognition in the *Guinness Book of World Records*, this being a Goliath Bird Eater (*Theraphosa leblondi*) who, on death, tipped the scales at four ounces plus. There is a species in Western Samoa, at the other end of the size scale, whose scientific name is *Patu marplesi*—the name, in type, is an enormous number of times larger than the spider, which is recorded as measuring 0.016" overall.

Theraphosa sp., *Pamphobeteus* sp., *Megaphobema* sp., *Xenethis* sp., *Acanthoscurria* sp., all are giants and usually described as Bird Eaters, which is slightly misleading, since they do not—as far as is known—eat large birds. The vision conjured to mind of a huge spider thundering through the jungle toting a blackbird-sized creature is almost cartoon-like. They will, in the wild, take hummingbirds.

The name 'bird-eating spider' was coined in the 17th century when an eminent French lady arachnologist was walking through the South American rainforests and came upon a fairly large *Avicularia* sp. devouring a nestling chick. Obviously, the spider had been prowling around her treetop home and had come upon the nest while the adult birds were away. Having managed to rob the nest, she had taken the spoils down to the ground, unusually, to eat, and was discovered and caught red-handed. Thenceforward, many large hairy spiders have been mis-termed 'bird-eaters'. It is true to say that the remains of small birds have been found in spider webs, but these are the webs of true spiders as opposed to theraphosid spiders.

A species newly arrived in the U.K. is the Kinani Rusty-Red Baboon Spider (*Citharischius crawshayi*), sometimes referred to as a 'Drumstick' Baboon. This species comes from Kenya and is now much sought after for its sheer size. For example, its carapace (head) can measure 33mm x 25.5mm and the abdomen is extremely large. Little is yet known about this spider that was first described by Pocock in 1900.

Therefore, it can be said that spiders come in all sizes, from microscopic to four-ounce giants. The small spiders' of Australia give grave cause for alarm since there is no doubt a bite from a Red Back (*Lactrodectus matctans haselti*) or a Funnel Web (*Atrax robustus*) can be almost lethal, although today there are anti-venins available worldwide. The Sydney Funnel Web (*A. robustus*) and the Tree Funnel Web (*A. formidabilis*) found from southeastern Queensland through the mountainous regions of northern New South Wales are to be avoided whenever possible. These spiders have taken up residence in gardens, under debris such as bricks, timber, tins and boxes; also under houses and out-houses. Along with the Red Back, both these demons lie in wait for prey and the Red Backs actually feed upon large skinks and housemice. More often they make do with the passing beetle and even other spiders. The Funnel Webs are termed Australian Tarantulas and belong to the mygalomorphs (tarantulas in general) although they are small. In New Zealand, the Red Back is known as Katipo and in America as the Black Widow. The male of the species (actually, there are several species of Widows) is unable to damage human skin since his fangs are not powerful enough to penetrate anything so tough, although this is not so with the female, who can do and has done incredible damage to human beings. About twelve deaths in Australia have been directly accredited to the Red Back spider,

Eurypelma californicus.

but the anti-venin
developed in 1956 is
effective if taken
within 80 hours of the
bite. In fact, it is
believed that some of
the deaths occurred
because the incorrect
anti-venin was given.

The Funnel Web
shows the opposite

venom potential since here it is the male that is more deadly. Nocturnal in habits, the main time of year when bites occur in humans is autumn, when the breeding season is in full swing and the male is searching for as many mates as possible. Thirteen deaths have been recorded from bites by the male Funnel Web. However, it has to be said in their defence that very few venomous spiders are known to court trouble, i.e., they will only attack if provoked. For example, in the days of outside sanitation in Australia, most of the bites from Red Backs occurred in the lower bodily regions! Wouldn't you bite if confronted with a rather large posterior?

PHOBIAS

The worst thing about any phobia is that those of us who don't have them find it difficult to understand those of us who do so suffer. Arachnophobia is a very popular phobia. It seems that 90 percent of humans are afraid of spiders. In my early days with spiders I found this very hard to accept; nowadays I hope I am more tolerant although I still cringe inside when someone says 'I can't stand spiders; they make me shudder'.

Even I, at an early age, was afraid of spiders. I really was very scared indeed. In fact, my earliest memory is of being four years old when one of neighbourhood tearaways put a spider down my neck, or so he said! In fact, he had not done so, but I was so hysterical that my poor mother had to strip me naked there in the garden to prove to me that the spider was not there! Even as a teenager, I was reluctant to go to bed if a spider was on the ceiling or the wall. My father would come along resignedly with his milk bottle and scoop the spider up to be taken away outside. Neither of my parents particularly liked spiders but they certainly never killed one.

A friend of mine was cured of arachnophobia with medical help that consisted of firstly showing black and white pictures in a magazine, progressing to a film with a spider in the background, then to a film with a spider in the foreground. The next stage is to have a live spider on a table top several feet away; then the spider is allowed to crawl on your hand while the patient watches. Gradually over a period of time, the spider can be touched by the patient, then held by the patient and finally put back into its tank by the patient. This method really worked.

A new process of

hypnotherapy is being tried and this can work extremely consistently as was proved on a television programme some months ago.

One theory is that arachnophobia is a deep-down fear passed on by our ancestors. Witness the legend of Little Miss Muffet, whose father forced her to eat spiders! Working upon cures for various diseases, Dr. Muffet tried out his experiments upon his daughter. The child, naturally, was terrified—hence the nursery rhyme. Another legend, although this one is probably true, was the irrational fear of Cardinal Wolsey, who was terrified of spiders to the point of hysteria. He would insist that his servants check his sleeping quarters at Hampton Court with the minutest detail being considered, before he would retire for the night. The spider in question became known as the 'cardinal' spider and, apparently, Wolsey was badly bitten by these spiders. Hence his fear.

So are these fears that become phobias real or is it all in the imagination? For many people it is REAL and for these we should have nothing but sympathy. For some people the fear is a pleasure; they enjoy being frightened of something or someone and no amount of medical help can

Little Miss Muffet, who sat on her tuffet. . .

change things. If a phobic wants to be cured then he/she can be, but it has to come from within the person and is not something which outside influences can make happen.

Research into fears and phobias shows a large difference between the two. One dictionary offers the following definitions for the two words:

PHOBIA: Fear, aversion, hatred, especially morbid or irrational;

FEAR: A painful emotion, excited by danger, alarm, apprehension of danger or pain.

Is there then such a vast difference, really, in definition, in meaning? A phobia is a fear but an irrational one, i.e., one that we are unable to clearly explain, whereas fear itself is of something or somebody of which or of whom we can clearly say 'I am afraid!'

It has to be said that one should exercise care in dealing with phobics; it has to be said that trying to cure a phobic without professional help could do more harm than good—very true, especially if unrelated medical conditions such as a weak heart exist. But then it must be right to attempt a cure in a controlled and sensible way.

The impression that most arachnophobics are female could not be further from the truth! In fact, in a recent radio phone-in many of the calls were from frightened men! It is a certain fact that 38% of the members of the British Tarantula Society are women, and of those circularized in a survey on creepy-crawlies in general some few years ago, those results clearly showed that women were far less afraid of spiders than men!

Brachypelma smithi, **Mexican Red Knee Tarantula.**

Epilogue

Now that you have read this book you have probably found some of your queries answered. Equally, you may well have more questions to ask. I welcome your letters c/o The British Tarantula Society, 81 Phillimore Place, Radlett, Herts., WD7 8NJ, England, and I will do my very best to help if I can. Please enclose a stamped addressed envelope for the reply. (Overseas enquirers should enclose an International Reply Coupon in the amount of first class airmail postage.)

To keep any animal in captivity, the best possible conditions must be created to ensure their comfort using a method of providing as natural as possible a habitat—this can be done!

I hope you have enjoyed this book.

Finally, may I express my most grateful thanks to Mr. Andrew M. Smith and Fitzgerald Publishing for allowing me to check habitat and location details in the *Tarantula Classification & Identification Guide*; and to Kathleen & John Hancock for their invaluable help on sexing theraphosids. Lastly, but by no means least, to Paul Carpenter for his wonderful photographs and Christine McNamara for her superb illustrations.

Further Reading

Browning, John G. *Tarantulas*. T.F.H. Publ., Neptune, NJ. 1981.

David, Al. *A Complete Introduction to Tarantulas*. T.F.H. Publ., Neptune, NJ. 1987.

Hancock, Kathleen & John. *Sex Determination of Immature Theraphosid Spiders from their Cast Skins*. Published by the authors, 28 Pump Mead Close, Southminster, Essex CM0 7AE, UK.

Lund, Dale. *All About Tarantulas*. T.F.H. Publ., Neptune, NJ. 1977.

Nichol, John. *Bites and Stings*. David & Charles, UK. 1986.

Smith, Andrew M. *The Tarantula Classification and Identification Guide*. Fitzgerald Publ.

Webb, Ann. *Wall to Wall Spiders*. Imprint Books.

Index